THE WAY
OF ACTING

THE WAY OF ACTING

THE THEATRE WRITINGS OF TADASHI SUZUKI

Translated by J. Thomas Rimer

THEATRE COMMUNICATIONS GROUP

Translation copyright © 1986 J. Thomas Rimer

Originally published in Japan as "Ekkyō suru Chikara,"
copyright © by Tadashi Suzuki

The Way of Acting: The Theatre Writings of Tadashi Suzuki is published by
Theatre Communications Group, Inc., the national organization for the
nonprofit professional theatre, 355 Lexington Ave., New York, NY 10017.

This book was supported in part by a grant
from The Japan Foundation.

Title page: The mountain home of the Suzuki Company of Toga.

Photographs by Katsuaki Furudate and Masaru Miyauchi.

Library of Congress Cataloging-in-Publication Data

Suzuki, Tadashi, 1939–
The way of acting.

Translation of: Ekkyō suru chikara.
"A play: Clytemnestra": p.
1. Theater—Japan—History—20th century—Collected
works. 2. Acting—Collected works. I. Suzuki,
Tadashi, 1939–   . Clytemnestra. 1986 II. Title
PM2924.S9713   1986   792'.0952   86-5894
ISBN 0-930452-56-9

Book Design by Joe Marc Freedman
Printed in the United States of America
First Printing June 1985
Second Printing December 1987
Third Printing June 1992

Contents

Preface

Tadashi Suzuki, one of the foremost figures in the contemporary theatre, has long been acclaimed, first in his native Japan, then in Europe and the United States, for the striking intensity, beauty, and communal energy of his theatrical productions. Those who have seen them will quickly surmise that behind the always powerful encounters that Suzuki engineers between his actors and his audiences lie both a philosophy of performance and a rigorous discipline that are unique. Those few fortunate enough to have worked with Suzuki in his actor-training classes either in Japan or in the U.S. know his method firsthand. This collection of essays written between 1980 and 1983, the first to be made available in a Western language, makes at least the outline of his ideas somewhat more portable—and accessible, at long last, to a much wider audience.

Suzuki's writings reveal the psychology of a thoroughly contemporary artist. Challenged to absorb ideas from a wide variety of sources, he works to create a powerful synthesis of the dramatic arts that, while altogether a part of its time, can draw fresh resonances from the accomplishments of Japan's great theatrical past. References to *nō* and *kabuki* are sprinkled through the book, but Suzuki's homage to the classics is both stronger and more heterodox than that of any other figure in the postwar

Japanese theatre. He has absorbed, then articulated, techniques and attitudes that serve the goals—not merely the superficial traditions—of the whole spectrum of Japanese theatre.

In none of the essays does Suzuki provide his readers with much in the way of autobiographical detail, but the outlines of his development emerge clearly. Suzuki began his work in the theatre in the 1960s, while still a student at Waseda University. His early plays and productions were political in nature and somewhat more consonant with the realistic styles of the mainstream Japanese theatre of that period, which drew on foreign models to create dramas addressing contemporary problems from a progressive point of view. After this initial phase, however, Suzuki's work began to take on more abstract and monumental qualities. During these years, too, he began to make use of the extraordinary talents of Shiraishi Kayoko, since proclaimed by many to be one of the great actresses of the world. In 1972, Suzuki and Shiraishi were invited by Jean-Louis Barrault to take part in an international theatre festival in Paris. Suzuki's recounting of his discovery in France of the power of the medieval *nō* theatre is one of the most evocative vignettes in this collection of essays.

The encounter with Barrault, Suzuki indicates, inspired him to examine the possibility of establishing a permanent stage, a spiritual home, for his company. This he finally accomplished in 1976, when he and his group moved from Tokyo to occupy a renovated farmhouse in the small village of Toga, in the mountains of Toyama Prefecture. Deep in that mountain country, which faces the Japan Sea and the continental land mass of Asia, Suzuki created a unique performing space; the philosophy behind its construction and use are beautifully articulated in various ways throughout the book.

Suzuki is also a shrewd and demanding critic of the contemporary world, and of Japanese culture in particular. His observations and comments reveal a sensibility all too well attuned to the dangers and ambiguities of the times in which we all live, whatever our nationality or cultural background. The attitude he adopts, more often than not, is one of wry despair, and his doubts seem as pertinent to the quality of life in the United States (which he understands very well) as they do for Japan. Still, much about the specifics of the arts in modern Japanese society can be learned from his critique, and in that regard, the book provides a unique glimpse into the workings of the theatrical world in Tokyo and elsewhere during the past two decades.

Those who read this book may be surprised to find that, despite Suzuki's fame as a teacher of acting, his training method is not described here in any precise detail. As he makes clear, however, that method can merely be *evoked* from the outside; true understanding of it can come only as one lives through and experiences his discipline. Perhaps it must even be lived through *before* it can be grasped intellectually. Suzuki's teachings are thus one with the methodologies used to train Japanese actors all the way back to the 1400s, when the rigorous and poetical teachings of Zeami on the *nō* first flourished. In this aspect of his thinking, Suzuki stands in the great line of Japanese teachers; and like the best of them, he is utterly unique.

Suzuki's writings, all redolent with his subtle modes of thought, are difficult to render into English because of their allusiveness and grammatical complexity. It is my hope that what has been translated here, whatever the shortcomings of the English version, will stimulate more interest in the work and thought of this vibrant and astonishing man, whose productions have created such admiration around the world.

I would particularly like to thank Peter Zeisler and Terry Nemeth of Theatre Communications Group for encouraging me to undertake the translation, and to express my great admiration for Laura Ross, my editor, for her extraordinary skill and patience in helping me revise the manuscript. Professor Yasunari

PREFACE

Takahashi of Tokyo University made a number of most helpful suggestions concerning details in the translation, thus improving both its smoothness and its accuracy. Finally, I would like to thank my friend, Mrs. Fumi Norica, for her encouragement and the many suggestions she made while I was working on my English version of the text.

J. Thomas Rimer
March 1986

THE WAY
OF ACTING

The Grammar
of the Feet

Despite the powerful influence of the Moscow Art Theatre on the mainstream of modern Japanese theatre, one of its leaders is known to have insisted that, in principle, Japanese actors should be performing dramas written in Japanese by Japanese dramatists. He insisted that a repertoire consisting solely of foreign plays in translation would never come to much. Why? The reason he gave was, "In the first place, our appearance is wrong; our arms and legs are too short."

The fact that doubts concerning the orthodox tradition in the modern Japanese theatre of faithfully reproducing foreign dramas was at least partially attributed to a shortness of arms and legs is interesting in itself. I myself don't think that the physical appearance of a Russian is automatically superior; still, it is true that the essence of a Chekhov production involves delicate reconstruction, in physical terms, of Russian manners and morality. Modern Japanese actors have gone to tremendous pains, throwing themselves into the effort of imitation, yet they have never achieved an appropriate likeness. So the failure has been attributed, quite bluntly, to the physiological: their arms and legs are too short.

Ever since the beginning of the Meiji period in 1868, there have been tremendous efforts within Japanese culture to catch up with, then surpass, the West. Although the actors have put themselves at the forefront of such activities, they have only managed to imitate the surface of things. If the above-mentioned expert meant to emphasize once and for all the obvious impossibility of remaking the Japanese physique, then he should be praised; he exhibited critical acumen in spotting the fundamental weakness in the West-oriented modern Japanese theatre. After all, it is better to see the truth as it is and abandon one's illusions, than to continue on while harboring a tremendous sense of inferiority. But those involved in the modern theatre movement have adopted the European mode too completely: the way to smoke, the way to use a handkerchief, the way to eat. "Louis Jouvet did this, Nemirovich-Danchenko did that, such-and-such film showed so-and-so." They have made an almost pathetic attempt to copy completely the surface of things.

Take as an example the performance in the role of Vincent Van Gogh given by Takizawa Osamu, the last of the famous actors who helped create the traditions of the modern theatre movement in Japan. In preparing the part he went all the way to France; he even walked on the roads along which Van Gogh had trudged. And when Takizawa heard that an old chair belonging to the artist had been found, he had a copy of it made and put on the stage. Yet the Van Gogh that the actor was to play was actually the one created by the playwright Miyoshi Jūrō in his *Man of Flame*. As Miyoshi himself is Japanese, and the Van Gogh he created was a part of his own thought, then his Van Gogh would not sit on such a chair. In fact, he might well sit on the floor, on a Japanese cushion. Yet, to the actors in our modern theatre, so anxious to recreate the illusion of reality, this kind of natural, unassuming approach would be seen as impossible. For them, if Van Gogh were to sit on a frayed and dirty cotton cushion, he would revert to being Takizawa Osamu and not the character he was playing. But, to me at least, a play such as *Man of Flame* can evoke only a Van Gogh who is nothing if not very theatrically Japanese.

If an actor really wants to perform in the foreign fashion, then unnatural makeup alone will not suffice; Chekhov's words will have to be spoken in Russian, or Shakespeare's in English. To go that far might be splendid indeed! In fact, however, we are stuck with playing *Uncle Vanya* and *Hamlet* in Japanese. In contrast to a number of other languages, Japanese has a pitch accent, and sentences can be inordinately long. For better or for worse, such is the language that Japanese actors must speak, a language grammatically constructed so that the listener cannot fully understand what is said until the end of the sentence, a language in which the verb comes last. Yet our actors try to gesture along with this language as though they were Russians, Englishmen, or Frenchmen. Gesture is tied intimately to the words being spoken; indeed, words *represent* human gesture. There can be no words spoken that are not intimately connected to bodily sensations and rhythms. Therefore, however long our arms and legs may grow, however our physical appearance may improve, no Japanese actor can imitate the Chekhovian manner as well as his Russian counterpart—as long as he is speaking in Japanese. The question of proper appearance has nothing to do with the real issue; it is a foolish premise in the first place.

The art of stage performance cannot be judged by how closely the actors can imitate or recreate ordinary, everyday life on the stage. An actor uses his words and gestures to try to convince his audience of something profoundly true. It is this attempt that should be judged. In these terms, most Japanese actors, whether their arms and legs are short, fat, or whatever, are capable of giving performances that might suit translated plays in quite another way. An actor, however long his arms and legs, will appear clumsy if he cannot project a sense of profound truth to his audience. The actor's nationality is immaterial. Of course Marlene Dietrich's legs are beautiful, but the stage is not the cinema. Nothing on stage enjoys the benefit of an appreciative closeup. Legs, even if they are fat and short, when perceived as part of the appearance of the actor's entire body, do not call attention to themselves. An actor can *create* a slender appearance; indeed, the creation of a desired appearance can serve as one definition of the art of acting. When a performance is truly effective, even a small actor can make an imposing figure—he can look even grander than the stage itself.

The way in which the feet are used is the basis of a stage performance. Even the movements of the arms and hands can only augment the feeling inherent in the body positions established by the feet. There are many cases in which the position of the feet determines even the strength and nuance of the actor's voice. An actor can still perform without arms and hands, but to perform without feet would be inconceivable.

Nō has often been defined as the art of walking. The movements of the actor's feet create the expressive environment. The basic use made of the feet in the *nō* consists of a shuffling motion. The actor walks by dragging the feet, turns around in a shuffle-like motion, and strikes a rhythm with his feet in the same way. The upper parts of his body are practically immobile; even the movements of his hands are extremely limited. Whether the actor is standing still or in motion, his feet are the center of interest. These feet, encased in *tabi* (white bifurcated socks) provide one of the most profound pleasures of the *nō,* as they move from a position of repose forwards and backwards, left and right, up and down with their own independent rhythm. Such patterns of foot motion can be created out of the intimate relationship of the feet of the actor with the surface of the *nō* stage. The very life of the art depends on the fixing and deepening of the relationships of the feet to the stage in order to render the expressiveness of foot movements all the more compelling. In fact, this kind of ambulatory art is involved in all theatrical performance.

Classical ballet, for example, is equally dependent on the feet, as is the traditional Japanese *kabuki*. In *kabuki* (except in the domestic plays, where the characters often sit), much of the audience's pleasure comes from watching the actors' foot movements, which are often more pronounced than in the *nō*. The *hanamichi* (the runway that connects the auditorium with the *kabuki* stage) is particularly well suited to emphasize the art of the feet.

Since the coming of the modern theatre to Japan, however, the artistic use of foot movements has not continued to develop. This is too bad, because realism in the theatre should inspire a veritable treasure house of walking styles. Since it is commonly accepted that realism should attempt to reproduce faithfully on the stage the surface manner of life, the art of walking has more or less been reduced to the simplest forms of naturalistic movement. Yet any movement on the stage is, by definition, a fabrication. Since there is more room within realism for a variety of movements than in the *nō* or in *kabuki,* these various ambulatory possibilities should be exhibited in an artistic fashion. One reason the modern theatre is so tedious to watch, it seems to me, is because it has no feet.

Since Japan's modern theatre attempts to take European drama and wed it theatrically to lifestyles of contemporary Japan, there is no room for the movements of bare or naked feet. Actors, because they must wear shoes to perform, have, in a manner of speaking, lost their feet.

When an actor puts on shoes, the movements of his feet are limited. Stamping, sliding, walking pigeon-toed, walking bowlegged—all of these are virtually denied him. When an actor does struggle to make such movements, the sinews in his ankle or his Achilles tendon will pain him, and his feet will develop blisters. Even in the West, specially designed footwear has been developed for the classical ballet which somewhat resembles the footwear used in the traditional Japanese theatre arts. Japanese *tabi,* which have served so long in that capacity, can still be put to good use on the stage today. We occasionally wear *tabi* in our everyday life, but they always suggest a certain formality. The modern theatre does nothing to promote the expressiveness of the feet; the feet are merely used as they are in ordinary life. In the *nō,* where ghosts serve as the protagonists, the art of the foot exists; but in the modern theatre, which purports to show living beings, there are none. How ironic, since in Japanese folklore the ghost is represented invariably as footless.

A performance begins when the actor's feet touch the ground, a wooden floor, a surface, when he first has the sensation of putting down roots; it begins in another sense when he lifts himself lightly from that spot. The actor composes himself on the basis of his sense of contact with the ground, by the way in which his body makes contact with the floor. The performer indeed proves with his feet that he *is* an actor. Of course, there are many ways in which the human body can make contact with the floor, but most of us, excepting small children, make contact with the lower part of the body, centering on the feet. The various pleasures that an actor feels as he comes in contact with the ground—and the growth in the richness of change in his bodily responses when he is in contact with the ground—constitute the first stage in his training as an actor.

In training the actors in my company, I have one exercise in which I have them stamp their feet in time to rhythmic music for a fixed period. Stamping may not be the most accurate term, for they loosen their pelvic area slightly, then move themselves by striking the floor in a vehement motion. As the music finishes, they use up the last of their energy and fall to the floor. They lie flat, in a hush, as though they were dead. After a pause, the music begins again, this time gently. The actors rise in tune with this new atmosphere, each in his or her own fashion, and finally return to a fully vertical standing position. This exercise is based on motion and stillness, and the contrasting expulsion and containment of bodily force. By means of strengthening breath support, this exercise develops a concentration of strength in the body.

The essential element in the first musical portion of this training exercise is the continuous pounding of the floor, using an even, unremitting strength without loosening the upper part of the body. If the actor loses his concentration on his legs and loins and so misses the sense of being toughened or tempered, he will not be able to continue on to the end with a unified, settled energy, no matter how full of energy he may feel. What is more, if the actor does not have the determination to control any irregularities of breathing, then toward the end of the exercise his upper body will of necessity begin to tremble, and he will lose the rhythm. In either case, the energy produced as the feet strike the floor spreads into the upper body. I ask that the actors strike the floor with all the energy possible; the energy that is not properly absorbed will rise upwards and cause the upper part of their bodies to tremble. In order to minimize such a transfer, the actor must learn to control and contain that energy in the pelvic region. Focusing on this part of the body, he must learn to gauge continuously the relationship between the upper and lower parts of his body, all the while continuing on with the stamping motion.

Of course, the idea that an actor can learn to control the apportionment of his energy, unifying it through his pelvic region, is hardly unique to my training exercises. All physical techniques employed for the stage surely involve such a principle. What I believe I have added, however, is the idea of stamping the foot—forcing the development of a special consciousness based on this striking of the ground. This concept arises from my conviction that an actor's basic sense of his physicality comes from his feet.

In ordinary life, we have little consciousness of our feet. The body can stand of its own accord without any sense at all of the relationship of feet to earth; in stamping, we come to understand that the body establishes its relation to the ground through the feet, that the ground and the body are not two separate entities. We are a part of the ground. Our very beings will return to the earth when we die.

It is often said that the concept behind my exercises is

somehow very Japanese, but I don't believe this is so. Even the classical ballet dancer who attempts to leave the ground behind altogether principally senses an intimate connection with the earth. According to the Dutch scholar Gerhard Zacharias, in his 1964 book *Ballet,* the most classic of ballet movements, the pirouette, is conceived of in the following terms:

> The pirouette is a symbol of the strength required to press down the foot. The foot that appears in a dream is that organ of the body that touches the ground, expressing the connection between the body and the surface of the earth. When one thinks of what the pirouette symbolizes, it is clear that the idea of the knee represents what is connected to the underground, to the sensual—consider the etymology *genu* (knee) and *genus* (sex). After all, the image of the knee for the Greeks did not suggest the worship of the gods on Mount Olympus; the knee was utilized to pay homage to the gods in the underworld. Sophocles has Oedipus, before he goes in death to the gods of the underworld, kneel and pray to the earth itself . . . in praying to the gods of the underworld, kneeling does not at all suggest devotion or service, but is rather an expression of attachment to them.
>
> The pirouette, in the classical dance, represents (in contrast to the usual academic explanations) the manifestation of a dynamic harmony, an equilibrium between height and depth, sky and earth, weightlessness and weight.

The traditional Japanese performing arts share this balance between height and depth, sky and earth. In the Japanese case, however, the equilibrium, the source of strength, emanates in all directions from the pelvic area, which radiates energy into horizontal space. This is why, while the upper body moves as far as possible upwards, the lower body attempts to descend in a kind of counter-movement. Thus the sense, established by the feet, of an intimate connection with the ground is all the more strengthened. The symbolic gesture of dragging the feet or of rhythmically stamping thereby reveals this sense of intimacy with the ground.

That profound student of Japanese culture Origuichi Shinobu (1887–1953), in his study of the Japanese traditional arts, drew attention to a consistent desire to strike a rhythm with the feet; this practice on the stage doubtless derives from the powerful foot-stamping originally used to magically ward off evil. If such is the case, the traditional playing space in the Japanese theatre can be defined in terms of the area it can provide for such movements. Vestiges of this can be found in the ancient dances still performed in the *nō* called *sanbaso,* which include the kind of foot-stamping that was designed to create a sense of peace and harmony as the performer moves around in a fixed space.

The series of movements I have designed, which range from falling down to standing up, begin with the rhythmical repetition of the stamping motions, in which the body, centering on the pelvic area, is made firm; movements of the upper part of the body are designed to send a gentle strength throughout the whole body. As the actor stands up, he moves like a puppet to the rhythm of the music. The exercise thus eradicates the ordinary, everyday sense of the body. Therefore, when the great majority of actors begin these exercises, the nuances in their movements disappear and they tend to move in a mechanical, constrained fashion. It has been my experience that American actors, involved as they are in realistic theatre, most often react this way. When they begin, they perform the foot-stamping movements with considerable strength, but they soon lose energy and begin to move in a vague and distracted way. From this they conclude that my exercises are somehow "Japanese," that Americans cannot perform them because their legs are, on the whole, longer than those of Japanese actors. When Americans grumble at the difficulties in performing these exercises, even some members of my troupe find themselves responding that American legs are too long. Yet there is absolutely no connection between these exercises and the length of an actor's legs. Nor is it a question of bodily strength. The exercises are intended as a means to discover a self-consciousness of the interior of the body, and the actor's success in doing them confirms his ability to make that discovery. The actor learns to become conscious of the many layers of sensitivity within his own body. A Japanese actor has no special claim to success, or to developing those skills in his own body, any more than anyone else.

The gesture of stamping on the ground, whether performed by Europeans or Japanese, gives the actor a sense of the strength inherent in his own body. It is a gesture that can lead to the creation of a fictional space, perhaps even a ritual space, in which the actor's body can achieve a transformation from the personal to the universal.

In the Yoshino area of Nara Prefecture, at the temple of Tokuzōji, there is a devil-chasing dance held late at night on the third of each January; it is called the *shishi-oi,* or the "wild boar chasing ceremony." The villagers, in bare feet, cry out a series of syllables, *chenyato, chenyato,* as they stamp fiercely with all their strength on the floor of the *Jizo* hall. The current generation of villagers seems to believe that the rhythm of such frantic stamping was originally intended as a means to drive away the wild boars coming to pillage the fields. According to *A History of the Traditional Arts in Japan,* compiled by the Research Society for the Arts, however, the word *shishi,* which the farmers take to mean "wild boar," is actually a corruption of the word "magician," *shushi.* In this interpretation, the reverberations from the pounding on the floor were originally intended to help chase evil spirits away, and possessed a magical significance in bringing such prayers to fulfillment. It seems to me, too, that the idea of making a great deal of noise in order to chase away wild boars can hardly account for the etymology of the word *shishi.* Perhaps there were some attempts, of course, to chase them away, but the boars can hardly have been the only objects of the farmers' efforts. There are many things that damage crops, some not necessarily visible to the eye. No doubt the original meaning of *shushi*—"magician"—is the applicable one. What interests me in this is not the etymology of the name, however, but the fact that the farmers pound their feet on the floor. From ancient times, pounding on the ground has constituted a ritual connected with farming. It served as a gesture to suppress those malign spirits that might bring harm to crops and to men. Later this ritual also became a charm to ward off actual predators, so that both functions were served at once.

In the book on the traditional arts of Japan mentioned above, a similar ceremony is described, which was given the same name. Until recently, it was performed in a place called Kuroyama in Okayama Prefecture. In that case, the floor was not stamped; rather, the wainscotting of the temple was daubed with clay and the participants pounded with all their might on those surfaces, using special sticks made of sumac wood. Such ceremonies of stamping and pounding seem to have been a part of Japanese ceremonial behavior since the beginning of our culture.

The *Shintō* goddess Ame Uzumi no Kami, who danced on an overturned bucket in front of the Heavenly Rock Cave, stamped and pounded with her stave in a kind of incantatory manner. The dance is often considered to represent the mythological beginnings of the *kagura,* the sacred *Shintō* dances. Origuchi Shinobu, in his *Six Lectures on the Traditional Japanese Arts,* says the following about the famous dance (as recorded in the *Kojiki* and other repositories of ancient Japanese legend):

> This overturned bucket can be said to represent the earth; it serves as a symbol of the ground. To stamp resoundingly on the earth, to pound on it with a stave, and to cry out, indicates that the soul, which has been sleeping inside the earth, lying concealed within it, or kept inside, can now come forth. The soul can now be released to join the other gods who are close beside.

The act of stamping and pounding not only signifies pushing down on the enemy, suppressing him or driving him away, but suggests as well the calling forth of the energy of an object of worship, the taking of that energy into oneself, the bringing to ripeness of that life energy. Such gestures can drive away evil spirits and bring about magical results, permitting the good spirits to come into the body of the performer with a strength greater than that of the bad. The many stamping gestures in *kabuki* and *nō* doubtless derive from these kinds of physical sensations. The traditional phrase "stamp in the six directions" can be interpreted to mean gesturing to the spirits, arousing that spiritual energy, confronting it, taking it into oneself. When the spirit has entered the one performing the gestures, that person in turn becomes brave and finds himself ready for deeds of strength and valor.

It is for such reasons that the classic Japanese dramas were often set in spots where such spirits were thought to dwell, the site of a burial, for example, or a raised grave mound. The construction of the *nō* stage, even as it exists today, includes empty jars implanted underneath the floor; the bottom of the stage is hollowed out. The purpose of this is not only the artistic effect of having greater reverberations when the actors stamp their feet. These sounds can also be understood as a means to help in the calling forth of the spiritual energy of the place, a summoning of the ancestral spirits to come and possess the body of the performer in a kind of hallucination. The very echoes produced stand as proof of the existence, through physical sensation, of a mutual response between actor and spirit.

This sort of sensation is necessary for performers on the stage, even today. The illusion that the energy which gives strength to one's own body can be received through the feet is altogether natural. It is our good fortune that *nō* actors have continued to act on the basis of this notion up until today. The gravesite or mound resembles the inside of the womb of a mother who has given birth; the surrounding surface represents the mother herself. So it follows that the performer's actions are based on the premise that he can transcend his individual self and perform, symbolically, for all mankind.

Zacharias has stated:

> In Kurt Sachs's *World of the Dance,* he has written concerning a dance for abundant crops, that there was a tribe, now vanished, in Tasmania that possessed a secret device for bringing rain. They threw themselves down and rolled on the ground, beating with their hands and feet. With this gesture they imitated the lightning and thunder with their own bodies; by analogy, they sought it out. Or they leapt up high into the air, guiding the energy of nature to the earth and thereby confining it in the ground. This ancient ritual seems to have existed in older German dance as well.
>
> When Moses left Egypt, he struck his cane into the rock at God's order and so found water. Forms of this ceremony of striking can be seen in the rituals of many cultures. The clapping of hands is one version, a gesture of worship widely observed. This striking can be seen as a gesture of giving birth, of the effort of pulling forth energy (the striking of a flintstone may suggest another analogy). In ballet, the concept of *battement* conveys the same meaning. It brings about the acquisition, then the release, of psychological and bodily energy.

In the communality of gesture that exists on a level beyond the specifics of cultural diversity, the lower half of the body and the feet always seem to be the operating parts of the body, rather than the upper portions. The feet alone can stamp and strike the earth, which represents man's unique foundation and authority. The feet have provided, up until now, the ultimate means of connection between man and earth.

Contemporary Japanese actors are required to play in a variety of styles (setting aside such forms as *nō* and *kabuki,* where

methods of performance, fixed long ago, involve a fixed repertoire). All kinds of stage language are employed, from dialogue
reminiscent of *kabuki* itself, to the kind of Japanese language
used when the text is translated from other languages; from the
most contemporary slang that mixes English with Japanese, to
the language of the drama of ideas, to that used in popular culture; from dialogues to long monologues. And words are not the
only element involved. In terms of movement, actors must take
into account Japanese-style costumes as well as Western dress.
They need to practice different kinds of motions, from the dancing needed for musicals to the absolute stillness required when
sitting on *tatami* matting in Japanese style. A committed actor
will try to master as broad a range of movements as possible. The
task is truly a difficult one, since audiences naturally expect to
witness a variety of skills on the stage. Then, too, as the style of
stage language changes, the actor's movements and his
psychological consciousness must alter. For a performance to
convey its full flavor to the audience, the proper relationship between the words spoken and the movements of the actor must
remain firmly established.

If, as in the case of the *nō* actors, the upper body is held
straight and remains still while the actor's voice is pressed out
from the abdomen to resonate through the body, the performer
cannot manage the kind of stage language used by such avant-
garde playwrights as Samuel Beckett or Eugene Ionesco, or by
such contemporary Japanese playwrights as Kara Jūrō or
Betsuyaku Minoru. The *nō* actor's body has been trained to
produce a kind of chanted vocalization employing a clear, bright
voice, a sound quite unsuitable for stage dialogue. Famous *nō*
actors perform only in the *nō*, without attempting other forms of
theatre. Most modern stage performers, generally speaking, are
not trained to the level of *nō* or *kabuki* actors. In fact, if a modern
actor did receive some kind of fixed training for the modern
stage, then he too would risk becoming a kind of *nō* actor, a new
kind of *onnagata* who could only perform circumscribed roles,

limited to one style from within the whole possible range of contemporary theatre.

Whatever the level of his training, an actor must continue to sharpen his consciousness of both voice and body. In a sense, a contemporary performer ends up being as busy as a person in a supermarket. He may have to know the traditional vocal techniques used in *nō* and *kabuki,* as well as those used in Western popular or operatic music; he needs a knowledge of traditional Japanese dancing techniques, modern dance, informal styles of *nō* dancing, even fencing. An actor cannot simply decide for himself what skills he needs. A look at the actor-training schools and studios in America as well as in Japan reveals the same diversity of coursework. It is as if training in all these areas needs to be available to prospective performing artists. But in my view, all this training should not simply be for the purpose of showing off an individual's talents as an actor. I see it more as a means of discovering the substratum that lies beneath the surface of these divergent styles.

Expression in the theatre does not merely consist of dance-like motions of the body. What makes the theatre theatrical involves all the variations of the body when speaking. I have attempted to examine closely all the postures used in a person's daily life, particularly when speaking. The words that we speak truly influence our physical situation, but there are a limited number of basic situations that can be observed in a finite number of combinations. The contemporary actor's first duty is to objectify those bodily situations, determine the emotional context that words will create under each set of circumstances, and then be conscious of these relationships.

What, then, are the basic postures involved in the conduct of our daily lives? To simplify the description, the body positions can be divided into two categories, those in which the body is still and those in which the body is moving. Stillness (leaving aside sleeping, of course) can be further subdivided into three groups: standing, sitting in a chair, and sitting on the floor. In a standing position, balance can be achieved on one leg, but usually one stands vertically on both legs. The sitting position varies depending on the way in which the legs are folded and the form of the chair, but one usually bends at the hips; as in standing, there is only one basic position. The most common position for a Japanese person is sitting on the floor, in its many variations. I have adapted the various divisions employed by Irisawa Tatukichi in his 1921 study *Concerning the Sitting Habits of the Japanese:*

Sitting on the Floor
(a) feet folded under the legs
(b) feet folded outside the legs
(c) cross-legged
(d) cross-legged with the palms of the feet turned up
(e) cross-legged with feet partially intertwined
(f) cross-legged with feet fully intertwined
(g) sitting with feet extended
(h) one leg crossed, one knee bent
(i) both legs bent
(j) squatting, legs hugged by the arms
(k) kneeling

There are various ways of sitting with both legs bent. This sitting position was adopted by noblemen in ancient times. The variant of kneeling on one foot can be seen in the *nō*. The squatting position is used when defecating, and squatting on the toes can be observed in *sumō* wrestling. All involve an opening motion of the knees. These, plus variations—sitting with the feet under the legs such as when sitting with the legs to one side, or kneeling when the hips are lifted—represent the total of five basic sitting positions on the floor, probably about all the possibilities.

Next come positions in movement, when the body shifts its

1. Feet folded under the legs.

2. Legs extended to the side.

*3. Cross-legged with feet fully
intertwined.*

4. Feet folded outside the legs.

5. Cross-legged with feet partially intertwined.

6. Cross-legged with the palms of the feet turned up.

7. Feet extended.

8. Cross-legged.

9. Both legs bent.

10. One leg crossed, one knee bent.

11. Squatting, legs hugged by arms.

12. A half-kneel.

13. *A variation on the squat.*

14. *Another variation on the squat.*

15. *Lifting the hips from the kneeling position.*

16. *Kneeling.*

WALKING

17. Walking pigeon-toed.

18. Shuffling the feet.

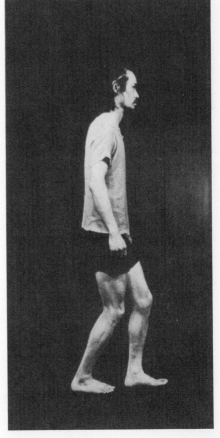

19. *Walking on the inside of the feet.*

20. *A bowlegged walk on the edge of the feet.*

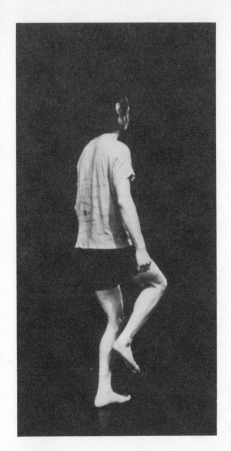

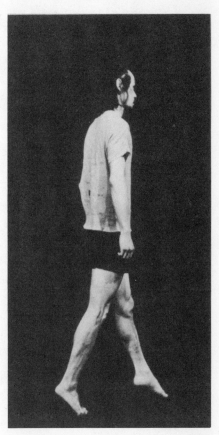

20. *Foot stamping.*

22. *Walking on the toes.*

23. *Training exercises.*

position. Usual modes of movement involve walking on both legs, but there are also movements made while standing and sitting. Movements made while standing can be described as follows: In an ordinary walking movement, the soles of the feet and the heels are lifted up and walking is performed by pushing off with the toes. This kind of movement is taken to an extreme by ballerinas and certain hooved animals. According to Kondō Shirō in his book *Conversations About the Feet:*

Animals that walk on their toes, such as dogs, cats, and other carnivorous species, do not touch their heels to the ground. They are able to walk comparatively quickly.

Hooved animals such as deer, goats, and horses also stand on their toes, which constitute the hoof, and so are able to move quite swiftly.

Animals that walk on the soles of their feet, such as rats, bears, beavers, and others, walk with their whole feet flat on the ground and so move comparatively slowly. Mankind, too, which belongs to the class of primates that walk with feet flat on the ground, stands on both legs and walks with a flat heel, a technique that represents something of a special means of movement even within this category.

According to this system of categories, hooves provide the fastest means of movement, particularly in running.

There is also a whole variety of movements used in walking: sliding the feet on the floor without lifting the soles from the ground; a slightly pigeon-toed walk such as that used by the *onnagata* in *kabuki,* in which the hips are slightly bent and the toes turned slightly inwards; moving with the toes turned slightly outwards, as in roller skating; walking bowlegged with the soles of the feet facing each other and partially positioned on edge; or walking sideways with a sliding motion.

Movements made while in a sitting position can be broken

down into three broad categories: crouching, shuffling on the soles of the feet, and crawling on the toes. These motions are used in defecation or in towing the mark in a *sumō* wrestling match, and can be observed in daily activities such as weeding a garden.

The three basic forms of movement are those performed while walking, standing, and sitting. But it must be remembered that human actions, whether they involve movement or not, flow in a continuum. For example, a person sitting with his feet under his legs may shift onto one knee, then stand on the soles of his feet, rise on his toes to take a book off of a shelf, then sit down to read.

How does an actor weave such bodily situations and physical movements into a connected series of motions? And how does he maintain the necessary physical equilibrium so that, without disrupting his breath control, he can vocally articulate the theatrical image he is striving for, whatever the stage language involved? Part of my training is based on a theory of how a contemporary actor can carry this out. Of course, a great performer will transcend any kind of practiced routine. The fact that these exercises may have some effect on an actor is no guarantee at all that he will become a superior performer. What I have developed is a kind of physical "grammar" for actors in performance, based on my own ideas. When people talk together, as it were, their grammatical meticulousness will not automatically ensure that they produce a *living* conversation.

Considering the various types of body placement from another perspective, changes in posture and movement often seem closely related to differences in the position of the feet. It is for this reason that this grammar, this way of using the feet, has been developed around the differences in sensations felt by the body as it connects with the ground. The goal is to ensure and enrich the histrionic unification of the whole bodily expression along with the speech; both these elements are constructed on the basis of the feet. The actor can thus have a different sense of existence on the stage than he does in ordinary life; he need not confront his body or his stage language in any feigned or empty fashion; both can function as one. In the fullest sense, he will have his feet on the ground. The value of my training can be said to begin and end with the feet.

In most of the housing now constructed for Japanese city living, and particularly in modern, Western-style apartments, there are no more hallways, no more wooden floors. Even if one can occasionally be found, the surface is carpeted and no bare wood can be seen. It is no longer possible to observe children or a wife down on all fours with a polishing rag. Vacuum cleaners have become the accepted method for cleaning. Yet the perception that our hands are also our feet, gained from a "floor-cleaning" kind of movement, is an important one. A child who experiences this will understand, even after growing up, that parts of the body other than the feet can have a dialogue with the ground. Why is it, I wonder, that architects have done away with this kind of space altogether?

Because wooden hallways and passageways have disappeared, the feet and hands of modern man have been separated from each other; we have forgotten that mankind is one of the animals. Space is now planned for multiple uses, for its functional possibilities; one area often has the same characteristics as another. In trying to construct an ideal living space using this "democratic" concept, spaces are profitably divided into squares—up, down, left, right, front, and back, all constructed from the same materials. It is perhaps for this reason that hallways have disappeared. Along with them, ceilings have disappeared as well; or, more accurately, since rooms have become boxes, each side of the box—including the ceiling—can perform the same function. Traditionally, a floor could never have become a ceiling. The idea of reversible surfaces in a living space has only become possible with the advent of modern architecture. The same principle can be observed, symbolically, in theatres as well.

In *kabuki* theatres constructed up until the end of the last century, a tower was built above the eaves or the front gate. This tower functioned as a means of announcing publicly the fact that theatrical performances were permitted, and it was thought that the tower represented the spot to which the gods descended. When entering the stage, actors faced the tower as well as the spectators, so that when they paid their respects to the audience, they did so to the tower as well. Just as in the classical ballet, the final bow was for the divine spectators who were said to reside behind the actual audience. The *hanamichi,* that raised passageway used in the *kabuki* theatre, was a space on which to perform for the gods, and a path on which to walk in order to pay one's respects to them. Virtually every modern theatre has removed both the raised passageway and the tower, leaving behind only a square, empty space. Thus, theatrical space, like living space, can now be turned upside down or backwards. Each side is the same.

Perhaps this shift is natural. Modern man no longer believes in gods he cannot see; in the theatre, the gods have become the members of the audience themselves. Any space that—though seemingly useless—could inspire a sense of the sacred, has now disappeared. The gods did not only descend into the towers of the *kabuki* theatres; they lived, invisibly, in empty spaces. Even now, if you made a trip deep, deep into the mountains, you would come across spaces that are fenced in but otherwise exhibit no special qualities. If you lingered there, some spirit or other might seemingly manifest itself in that space, and you might suddenly find yourself in tears. This relic of the traditional Japanese susceptibility to space can still be found in *Shintō* shrines or on the *nō* stage. Nowadays, though, however many tears you might spill, that space is empty, worthless. There seems no longer any reason to build a path to it; similarly, modern theatres have abandoned any attempt to construct connecting

passageways to the gods. Towers, *hanamichi,* the bridge onto the
nō theatre, all have been abandoned.

So it is that however colorful a modern play may be, it loses an
inner profundity, and the art of movement is diminished as well;
its feet are somehow not on the ground. Perhaps that is why the
modern realistic drama, which used to seem "new," now seems
"old" in the eyes of the younger generation. Of course I do not
advocate that the gods be called back again into the contemporary theatre. Still, I cannot help but feel that, at the least, we
would benefit from a rampway or two, on which we could really
exercise our feet to prevent physical deterioration.

In the theatre built for my company at Toga-mura, the stage
consists of two walkways which themselves serve as the playing
spaces. In between the forward and rear walkways, a flexible
partition-like structure is installed. Depending on whether it is
open or closed, various entrances and exits can be established.
When the door is completely shut, only the forward area can be
used as a performing space. When the partition is removed altogether, both ramps can be used at the same time.

The stage and the theatre are built of wood in the style of
Japanese mountain farmhouses with their steeply pitched roofs.
Four central pillars rise up to support the structure and, at a
glance, the performing space may seem to resemble that of a *nō*
stage. Many visitors, in fact, remark on this, perhaps because of
the placement of the central pillars. Actually, the construction
and layout of the stage are altogether different. The *nō* stage has
a central playing area. The actor enters from the bridge; after he
crosses it, he walks into an empty space that represents the acting
area. Once he steps onto the bridge he must eventually leave by
that route as well. On our Toga stage, however, there are no such
structures attached to either the left or the right wings of the
stage. No matter where an actor enters, he can exit freely in any
direction he chooses. There is thus no restricted "main stage" or
"rear stage" as in the *nō;* our playing space is designed for a continuous flow of movement. It is this kind of flowing space that I

have dubbed a "passageway." The protagonist of a *nō* play usually appears for a short time, and from the grave; when he has finished his business on earth, he must return from whence he came. He would be in trouble without a proper destination! It is my view, however, that a modern man, who has no place to call his own and whose gods have departed, lives best on the kind of stage I have constructed. All of us, at all times, everywhere, now seem to live a life composed of passages.

2

House and Family

I once heard the following story from my former friend and colleague, the late *nō* actor Kanze Hisao. It seems that right after the war there was a millionaire in Japan who asked if the Kanze family, the "House of Kanze," if you will, would be willing to sell its name to him. It was not a question of the "house" as architecture, but as a famous name. Of course, when Hisao was active, the family did have a magnificent stage installed on its property, and I suppose that it would have been included in any sale. But the real goal of the millionaire was to buy the actual name of the family. I had heard of the titles to the old Japanese peerage being sold, but not the name of a famous family. And it wasn't as if it were the name of a store, or of some trademark; the name Kanze had stood for many centuries as the symbol of a family devoted to the performing arts of the *nō*.

Unlike actors in *kabuki,* artists who perform the *nō* employ no financial managers, and so their livelihood was extremely precarious just after the end of the war. Public opinion underwent an enormous change at that time. For many, it suddenly seemed that the *nō* was a useless art, valuable only because it was old. I suppose that the millionaire must have thought that he could buy himself someone else's glory. Did he want to call himself a "Kanze" in order to get up on the stage and dance himself?

Or did he think of a way to use the name to pull in more money? In any case, his idea was certainly a novel one.

When I heard the story from Hisao, I thought it merely amusing and laughed about it. But, funny though the incident may be, it set me to thinking about a number of things. For one, Hisao's very family name, Kanze, derives from the development of his art; his actual family name is Oribe. He belongs to the secondary line of the Kanze family, which was established in 1752 by Oribe Kiyohisa, the younger brother of the inheritor of the main branch. If the Kanze name were sold, would Hisao have to go back to using his ordinary family name of Oribe? Would he be forced to use another artistic name while performing on the stage? Or could he sell the name of his branch of the family only? And how could the sale actually be accomplished? Thinking it over, the comical problems seemed endless.

I remember reading an article at some point or other to the effect that the *kabuki* actor Nakamura Utaemon had decided to stop using his name merely on a personal basis; he wanted to register it as a trademark. What this means, I suppose, is that Utaemon was afraid that someone might appropriate his stage name. In the case of Kanze Hisao, however, there are really no cogent reasons for registering the family name. After all, the name Kanze is not used at all in the same fashion as a *kabuki* actor's is; and over the years it has more or less come to function as the family's real name. Leaving aside the legal technicalities, though, that millionaire could certainly have taken the Kanze name and used it as his own. After all, if bloodlines were not the issue, someone could even style himself as the Emperor; by that definition, using the Kanze name would certainly be a possibility. Actually, Hisao told me that he once laughed when, walking around in Kyoto, he saw a shop curtain in front of a modest little restaurant with the name "Kanze" written across it.

What then would be the formalities required in the process of actually selling a name? In *kabuki* literature, particularly in the plays of Tsuruya Namboku (1755–1829), there are many characters who live, die, join together, then disappear, all because of the fate of treasures that belong to and so symbolize the family name—a scroll, a precious manuscript, or whatever. In such dramas, when a family treasure is lost, the very existence of the House is affected. One could therefore deduce that the family name is sold away precisely at the moment when such a family treasure is turned over to a buyer; an emblem is handed over that appears to symbolize the spirit of the family.

In the case of Namboku's work, this "spirit" refers to that of the founder of the family name. Traditionally, "ancestor" in this context does not indicate the most remote forebear one can trace in the biological sense; rather, it refers to the individual who actually founded the family name. The descendant who puts himself in charge of ceremonies and observances honoring this ancestor thus proves himself to be, as it were, the authentic descendant. This person usually possesses some calligraphy in the hand of the ancestor or some object owned by him: the family's treasure. The spirit of the ancestor somehow adheres to, or is manifested in, this scroll, this object, and can thereby provide some form of protection to the ensuing generations.

In the historical *kabuki* plays, these treasures are received as gifts from the house of the master whom the ancestor had originally served; thus, should something happen to a family treasure, there was fear that the connections within the entire family line would be severed altogether.

The main branch of the Kanze family stretches back all the way to Kan'ami (1333–1384), the father of Zeami (1363–1443), who first perfected the *nō* theatre. Hisao's family treasure is doubtless some object received from that main family, something connected to Oribe Kiyohisa. One wonders, though, if his family is actually still in possession of such an object.

This separate, secret teaching concerning the art of the *nō* is crucial to our family and should be passed down to only one person in each generation. For example, even where the rightful heir is concerned, should he be without the proper abilities, this teaching must not be given to him. It is written that "a house does not mean merely lineage. Carrying on the line correctly defines a house. Succession is not a question of being born into the family, but of a real grasp of the art." This teaching can provide the means to come to truly master that exquisite Flower that permits the understanding of myriad virtues.

This is a section of Kan'ami's teaching as recorded by Zeami in his *Fūshikaden* (*Style and the Flower*). Zeami stresses that the family line is one of skill rather than of blood ties. To put it another way, in the case of Kanze Hisao, "Oribe" represents the bloodline, but "Kanze" does not. In the views of Kan'ami and Zeami, the family treasure is represented by the body of their very art itself. Therefore, the only one who can truly pay homage to the spirit of his ancestors and who can represent the essence of the family name is the one who possesses the art within himself, regardless of bloodlines. Possession of some sacred object has no bearing. To put things more simply, artistic skill represents the crucial link within the house. This logical and very lonely dream of an artistic communality represents a concept of lineage, of community, that Kan'ami and Zeami wished to create, or were perhaps driven to construct.

Of course, such a construct does not prohibit blood ties. Indeed, the fact that long lines of acting families continue to exist indicates that no other satisfactory means has been found to develop so many well-trained and gifted actors. Nevertheless, the conviction that a family line must be carried on through the art itself remains. And it is true that Kan'ami's dream of a communality of art, though considered a very radical concept in his day, was practical as well. Yet the kind of artistic "family" we now witness in Japan seems to have removed itself from the realm of artistic accomplishment, transforming itself into an association with an economic concept of art unique to Japan, the *iemoto* or Family Master system. What is more, the fact that this Family Master system solidified itself between the latter part of the nineteenth century and the end of the last war is proof of how powerful the very concept of "family" has been as an organizing principle of Japanese society during the country's modernization. These days, few people consider the fact that the Master should be the one who is able to lead his art; they only know that somehow or other the concept of a proper Master involves the need for a suitable symbol connected to the practical administration of the group. There seems no necessity for name and reality to match. Actually, the current Family Master of the main Kanze school of *nō* is an adopted son; and although surely not a supreme master of his art, he does lead his troupe very well indeed, and so serves as an excellent example of how things stand in regard to lineage in contemporary *nō*.

Because the artistic significance of "family" has thus become unclear, it is not inconceivable that our millionaire, with no blood ties to Kanze and virtually no experience on the stage, came to believe that, were he to assume the economic support of the troupe, he could become Master of the family. He was evidently a practical man of action and was not interested merely in buying the glory of a centuries-old tradition. Rather, in offering to purchase the right to run a family group, he proved himself to be a pioneer in the practical, materialistic spirit that has since brought into being Greater Economic Japan. So it was that Kanze Hisao, for his part, wished to remove himself from a family that had become locked into such a system. He was an actor who wished to return to the spirit of Kan'ami.

In my view, the *nō* as a form of theatre possesses four characteristics that define its unique existence. The first concerns the fact that, from the rehearsal period down to the actual performance, virtually no energy that is not human goes into an artistic creation. Non-human or inert energy is that which is created not by men or by animals but by electricity, oil, even by atomic power. The contemporary theatre tends to'increase its expressive abilities by the use of such inert energy. Even *kabuki* which, like the *nō,* is a premodern form of theatre, proves no exception. Its revolving stage, traps, lighting, even its music, all make some use of inert energy created by modern means. *Nō,* on the other hand, sustains its performing space with a minimum of electric lighting. The musical accompaniment, the chorus, the masks, the costumes, and the movements of the actors themselves are all projected through a natural craft. *Kabuki* cannot compare to the *nō* in terms of the human energy expended on the stage. There is one breed of sociologist who would compare the amount of inert energy used in a nation's manufacturing processes to the amount of physical energy used, so as to judge how advanced that country has become. If you apply that logic to the theatre, *nō* certainly remains a premodern form of art.

The second characteristic is that the *nō* is non-realistic in its expression. In the established structure of many *nō* plays, the dream of a priest wandering about the country on a pilgrimage summons up a person long dead, who plays out again a life already lived; the drama makes use of the realm of reverie and consciousness. This world consists of what cannot be seen or heard in everyday life, only what can be felt, absorbed. Such things are conveyed to the audience through a kind of vocal production and gesture that cannot be heard or witnessed in everyday life. The spectacle that unfolds on the stage is in no way a realistic portrayal of ordinary human characteristics.

The third point is that the environment in which the whole of the *nō* exists is altogether fixed. However diverse the real world may be, there is surely no other form of art which is so entirely predetermined. True enough, there have been exceptional occasions when *nō* actors have performed their repertoire outside the traditional stage environment. But such moments have been rare indeed; it is safe to say that when *nō* is enacted, it is on the stage created for it. Indeed, that stage itself constitutes an important element in the whole art.

The fourth characteristic involves the nature of *nō* perform-ance: even if a *nō* actor, in the middle of his role, falls dead on the stage, the performance continues. In the modern theatre, or even in *kabuki,* such a thing cannot be imagined. If an actor cannot continue, the curtain is drawn; the manager usually comes out to explain the situation to the audience, apologizing for the inter-ruption. But in the *nō,* if the *shite,* the main character, finds him-self unable to continue, he is immediately replaced by the *kōken,* the assistant. It is not altogether clear when this practice of substitution started, but the custom has prevailed since the be-ginning of the Meiji period (1868). Perhaps the explanation for the practice lies in some tradition of religious ceremony, in which the order of the performance must not be disturbed whatever happens to the participants; the program must be completed as planned. In any case, the performance of *nō* today incorporates unique methods. Whatever the logic that gave birth to such a form of theatre, the system has long been established.

I see these four points, then, as characteristics unique to the *nō.* Tendencies toward the first two of them, however, can be seen in the avant-garde theatre developed around the world since the 1960s. The use of human energy has been touted as a means to rehabilitate the actor; some feel that inert energy weak-ens the actor's effectiveness, drying up the real force of the drama itself. Grotowski led the movement in this direction. This kind of vision, that seeks a return to fundamentals in the face of a society ever more mechanized, has become less and less a unique property of the *nō.* For that matter, the theatre of ancient Greece was also performed outdoors and involved only human energy, thus rendering the first characteristic not altogether unique to Japan. Still, there are very few forms of theatre that break as completely as the *nō* with the use of such artificial energy.

The question of non-realism, as well, in light of the various

techniques that have been developed within the avant-garde theatre, cannot be said to belong only to the *nō*. After all, most
forms of avant-garde theatre unite in a repudiation of realism. In
that regard, these other forms resemble the *nō*. And although the
nō employs an ancient vocabulary, makes use of masks, and incorporates folk elements into its gestures, these elements cannot
be said to provide an altogether unique form of theatrical experience either. After all, ancient performance techniques celebrat-
ing the repose of the dead with singing and dancing revealed a
commonality that transcended individual folk customs and are
thus certainly not peculiar to the *nō*.

Strictly speaking then, the truly unique features of the *nō* are
those third and fourth points I made above: the fact that it is
performed in a unique playing space, and the fact that a performance cannot be interrupted even if one of the performers dies.
An examination of these two characteristics can reveal a great
deal about the relationship of *nō* to the commonality inherent in
the theatre. Indeed, it seems to me that the *nō* does suggest a
unique resolution to the issue of commonality that is inevitably
confronted when the theatre as a communal enterprise, surpass-
ing time and space, attempts to establish its finite existence. In
another sense, the third point can be related to the commonality
of the actors' physical bodies, while the fourth speaks rather to
their spiritual commonality.

The eminent folklorist Yanagita Kunio (1875–1962) has
written:

> The Chinese character used to write the word *family* can
> be pronounced two ways in Japanese, *ie* and *ya*. The history
> of the word is not altogether clear, but it does seem certain
> that the meaning of *ie* and *ya* [house; shop] are by no means
> identical. The idea of a house certainly suggests a covering
> or shelter, a structure that guards against the rain and the
> dew. Thus the word *miya* [shrine; literally the honorific *mi*

plus *ya*] is certainly intended to represent one such structure. A family, on the other hand, represents something different, a point of inner centrality. As a proof of this, to alter slightly the verbal expressions involved, the *e* of *ie* has sometimes represented "door" and can also signify "oven." This syllable *e* might well be defined as that thing central to the home, the fire that is placed in the middle. The whole idea of an oven may be looked on as a mere commonplace today. But in ancient times, all the family members would gather in the central room and eat together, in the largest available space. The oven or cooking place represented the spot where they gathered, and where they worshipped their gods.

A house, on the other hand, suggests an opposite connotation. Even a small structure with a roof that can keep off the rain and the dew can easily qualify. In general, "house" in the sense of *ya* suggests part of a larger family, or *ie;* many *ya* may come under that larger covering. We tend to get confused because the same Chinese character is used to stand for two different concepts: a single house (*ya*) and a whole group of families (*ie*). The chief reason that these two differing concepts have blended together and are written with one character has to do with technical developments in architectural construction.

(from "The Concept of the Term 'House'")

The point that Yanagita is making, when applied to the *nō* theatre, is a profoundly striking one. In his terms, the House can be explained as the stage that ensures the commonality of the physical performance of the *nō* actors, while the Family represents a concept which, relying on the logic of blood ties, provides for the establishment of a truly collaborative group represented by the family name. Therefore, according to the double usage of the word "family" as established by Yanagita, the *nō* is the dramatic form that can bring these special characteristics to life. Indeed, one could argue that it is the idea embodied in the subtitle of the book in which Yanagita's essay appears, "The house one can see and the house one cannot see," that serves to empower the *nō*, signaling its uniqueness as a form of world theatre.

When I was a student, the first night that I stayed at a friend's house, I frequently banged myself up rather badly. This kind of accident occurred particularly often in the winter. Because I suffered some kidney trouble, I would often hurry to go to the nearby bathroom but in the dark I would always bump into chairs, posts, and so on. The reason I got so many bruises in the winter was that I was always trying to get back into bed as fast as possible so as to be warm and relaxed all the sooner. But I always felt sorry later. Ever since I bumped into a post and gave myself a really nasty crack on the head during my college days, I have felt an inevitable sense of anxiety when staying in a place where the bathroom is too far removed from the bedroom. Sometimes, when the mother of one of my friends would hear about the problem, she would kindly leave a light on, but in most cases people would kindly turn it out. Trying to brazen it out, I'd tell them to forget the hall light, so as not to spoil their sleep; but I'd end up spoiling it anyway because, knowing that my sense of malaise was sure to take over, I would pace the hall between the bathroom and the bedroom, wishing for my bed at home, so conveniently placed.

After I had remained in any particular room for about a week, I found that my body came to know where things were located in the dark, and what movements were likely to push me into a wall. I seemed to gain some special skill at this. I didn't interpret this as proof of any special sensibility on my part; still, no matter how dark it was or how suddenly I needed to flee from the room, I always knew that I could find the door unless I was totally drugged with sleep. Curiously enough, once I developed that self-confidence I was able to sleep quite calmly.

That week before I could settle down always remained an unpleasant one, though, for I never had the sense that my body actually belonged in the room. My body didn't seem to be my own; it was something foreign, cold, a borrowed ornament, and I would find myself quite uncomfortable. There were times when, even after my body had become accustomed to the space and did seem to belong in the room, I still could not lose my sense of discomfort. Sometimes the problem arose from the arrangement of the space, or from the sort of wood from which the walls were made, or the decorations on them. In any case, it was not so much a question of my body not fitting in as the sense that there was something in the room that went against my deepest nature.

Now, this kind of occurrence in daily life suggests to me a series of problems that confront actors in the contemporary theatre. For example, an actor who is accustomed to performing in a narrow theatrical space with a capacity of, say, two or three hundred, who has suddenly to appear on a large Tokyo stage, cannot perform in the same fashion before a large audience in such an expanded area. With a week or so of extra rehearsal, the adjustments can be made, but such a loss of time is seen as uneconomical by any theatre company or entrepreneur. Usually, one day is considered sufficient and if any more time seems needed, the actor's status as a professional may be called into question; the producer will grumble, "What has all that rehearsal up until now been good for, anyway?" Actually, if the performers have really accustomed their bodies to playing in a small space, there is no reason why they should be able to adjust themselves to a different and larger space during one day's rehearsal. In fact, if the actor is sensitive to such physical relationships, it is normal for him to feel quite uneasy. Further, if he *can* adjust himself to a large space in one day, then just how good a job has he been doing on a smaller stage? Such a quick change would seem to provide proof of a body insensitive to the space around it. In the world of the contemporary theatre, it seems harder and harder to encounter a performer who can really take on this struggle in any substantial way.

Many actors and other theatre people feel that, because big theatres use microphones anyway, the difference between a small stage and a big one involves quantitative levels of sound or sight. They are convinced that the problems can be easily regulated mechanically. When such attitudes prevail, many actors who are in possession of their physical selves when performing in a small theatre lose themselves altogether on a large stage. As the artist cannot fit himself into the larger space, he is not "in his element." He cannot send out his own energy into every corner of the theatre so as to be able to then pull together all the spatial energy available to him. More likely than not, such an actor will find himself struggling earnestly on, allowing his audiences to see him and hear him so that his presence will somehow serve to symbolize his effort. But he will not be able to give the audience any sense of a character who possesses real depth. Cases like this are all too typical, and in such circumstances, the true physicality of an actor's voice and gestures are lost.

In a performance, then, it is not a question of making the voice and gestures bigger, like enlarging a photograph. The actor must give real life to his role by mastering and taking possession of the unique environment in which a performance must always live. Any actor who makes light of the fundamental physical relationships within the theatre space will discover that the matter of acting space becomes his most fundamental problem. The modern theatre has yet to work out a successful plan to deal with this problem. On this point, at least, the *nō* does have a real solution to offer, as shown by the very nature of the *nō* stage itself.

It is thanks to the properties of the *nō* stage that performers can continue dancing even when the lights are extinguished; there is no need for them to stop even if they find themselves blinded, as it were. The bodies of these actors have been trained to accustom themselves to that particular stage space ever since they were children, and their gestures reveal a command of that space. If modern actors were to perform on a *nō* stage, I wonder how long they could continue if the lights went out?

Now, think of actors performing in modern drama who take a play on tour, going from one size theatre to another. Their sense of a playing space is determined altogether through a consciousness gained by sight; darkness thus becomes the most frightening of possibilities for them. If they were to continue on in the dark, they would probably fall off the stage or bump into one another. Sudden darkness would falsely enlarge each individual actor's sense of the space around him. *Nō* actors never really have these kinds of problems. Thanks to their fixed playing space, they never feel any discrepancies in their own personal physical responses to that space. A *nō* troupe, trained to be as homogeneous as possible, assures this unity through the physical training provided its actors.

The works of novelists, artists, and composers are provided their essence by their sole creators. Such is not the case in the theatre. The theatre is what it is because various performers occupy the same space, living at that precise moment in a collaborative creation. *Nō* is presented in a place where the means for such collaborative creation are fixed, assumed; and on the basis of that assumption, an individual drama can be created, a world of illusion. In the modern theatre, on the other hand, actors do not recognize the need for such a fixed, communal performance space as a basis for their creation. They seek, rather, to depend on something spiritual, on psychological movement. In fact, the unity within many of the modern theatre troupes in Japan lies in their political ideology, a common emotional response to the charisma of a director, or in a sympathy developed toward the personal illusionary world created by a particular playwright. It is surely for such reasons that the modern theatre movement in Japan, with a history of almost seventy years behind it, has managed to realize only two or three special and personalized worlds—based on connections with specific playwrights—but has never managed until now to create a real ensemble for performance.

I certainly do not believe that the whole purpose of the theatre lies in the creation of some fixed ensemble that always exhibits the same characteristics and so perfects an art of performance. Such perfection would not necessarily be a good thing. Nor do I insist that it is necessary to create a form of contemporary theatre that rivals the *nō* in its ability to establish a commonality among its members by developing in them a common level of physical ability. The modern theatre cannot simply imitate those profound, sometimes disturbing insights created by the *nō* to project its image of physical mankind. We are our own contemporaries and so our psychological and physical movements do not naturally blend together; we show the discrepancies of our time within ourselves. The world of modern literature depends on such psychological movement and so allows us to grasp the reality of this human slippage. The *nō,* on the other hand, begins with the expulsion of any expression based on psychology and individual personality; it insists on a commonality that risks no dispersion. The fact that *nō* has shown that this is possible is cause enough for astonishment.

One often hears that physical training alone should be emphasized in the *nō,* and how, for example, an actor who has read Zeami's *Style and the Flower* only to be scolded sharply by his teacher, is then told, "Skip the theory; just watch what I do and copy it!" The *nō* actor Kita Roppeita, in conversation with the noted playwright Kinoshita Junji, dismissed the psychological aspects of the roles he played in the *nō* by saying, "Well, when I was a kid, when I raised my hand, I might have put it up a little too high. Or I might have stuck my foot out a little too far. But after doing this sort of thing for years and years, I just naturally became Benkei, [the monk who plays such a famous role in the classic *nō* play *Ataka,* the model for the celebrated *kabuki* play *Kanjinchō*] all by myself!"

Still, *nō* cannot be understood as a simple passing on of physical formalities, nor is it merely a manifestation of feudal psychological attitudes. The form, the shape of a theatrical performance, does not exist by itself; and if it is merely turned into a skill for its own sake, it will degenerate and vanish. Had this happened to the *nō,* there certainly would have been no *kabuki* to succeed it. In order for the *nō* to have developed in all its grandeur, there had to lie behind it the existence of a fixed, decidedly communal playing space. Miss the significance of this fact and you will understand nothing else of the art of the *nō.* That sense of communality is developed through the memory of just such a physical playing space; and although the actors are looked on as teachers, it seems unlikely that their art could have developed in a space that was any different.

The basis for this conviction lies not in gesture but in the space itself. These artists have never said that their art was based on this or that performance technique. But when a performance reaches the highest level it is because the teachers tend to explain themselves in quite specific terms, and the specificity of their explanations in turn becomes a means to explain, in terms of physical training, how to acclimate one's body to the space of the *nō* stage. There is an enormous difference between the assumption that performing skills develop of themselves and the conviction that such skills are indivisible from the place in which they are performed.

It is usually said that *nō* and *kabuki* are classical theatre arts. In my own view, both are in some ways more contemporary than our newest theatrical ventures. In the sense that the *nō* possesses its own unchanging completeness, regardless of its historical context, it exhibits more of the true qualities of a classic form than the *kabuki.* Because the environment in which the actors perform is fixed, that "environmentalization" of the acting which the eminent biologist Imanishi Kinji refers to as a "partition for survival" can be beautifully realized on the *nō* stage.

The adaptation of a living organism to its environment requires specialization. An organism that possesses no special tools will often be forced to reconstruct its physical appearance. As a result, a balance is struck: an organism that responds positively in one environment cannot do so in another. Thus the only path left open to the organism is to develop those requisite special features that will permit adaptation to a new environment. Such is the price paid by the organism for its evolutionary characteristics.

All living organisms behave in this fashion, adapting themselves to their respective special environments, and should they become masters of them, the world composed of these organisms, because of its "partitioning for survival," will be a world in which all creatures can live together in peace.

Imanishi Kinji, *My Theory of Evolution*

Because the *nō* stage environment has been thoroughly assimilated by its actors, individual performances need not be abstracted and stand alone; more important, actors have come to be made aware of their own physical presences. A truly great *nō* performer is one who would find it difficult to perform in the environment of any other playing space, a man who has truly absorbed his own performing environment. Where to stand? The pillars of the *nō* stage are visible to the bodies of the actors. Precisely because of this physical certainty, modern viewers tend to regard these actors as inhabiting some sort of sacred space.

This perception does not simply arise because of a pine tree painted on the back wall of the stage, where the gods are to descend, or because the *nō* stage can be described in somewhat the same terms that Mircea Eliade uses to describe a sacred space: a place where there is a possibility of moving from the territory of one universe to another. The fact that the *nō* stage has an entrance bridge leading from the greenroom is not the issue, nor is the fact that the performances of these actors originated in songs and dances for the dead. Rather, what is important is that because the bodies of the actors themselves can remember the indivisibility of the space in which they perform, they seem to have the ability to make a rent, an opening in that homogeneity. Because of their physical deviations from the movements of every-day life, the actors' bodies somehow seem equipped with some means to defy those amorphous and sterile perceptions of space that have evolved as modern culture has developed.

At the time of Kan'ami and Zeami, the *nō* represented a contemporary theatre. This theatre constantly renewed itself, serving as a proxy for the desires of its spectators. Doubtless, it touched on the sacred; but since it was born out of a popular spirit, the theatre must have fulfilled its sacred function in a suitably theatrical fashion. The actors performed outside, on a stage without a bridge, without a greenroom. The *nō* probably became a classic theatre and took on its aura of the sacred in the Tokugawa period (1600–1868), when it became highly ritualized and the Houses of *nō* were fixed once and for all. At the time when the *nō* was fixed in order to ensure commonality of physical performance, it gained a means to ensure its cohesion as a theatrical form. At the same time, however, a phase of degeneration set in; the fact that the repertoire of productions was completely codified is one of the unfortunate outcomes. I personally would be the last person to indulge in admiration for the *nō* simply as a splendid example of Japan's cultural history. But even so, I cannot help but marvel at a theatre that has bent the terrifyingly powerful concept of a House to its own purposes, and continued its life right down to the present.

In the suicide note left by Shimada Mitsuhiro, the executive director of the Nissho Iwai Company who supposedly held the key to the Lockheed airline scandal, he evidently wrote, "Our company is eternal." From my point of view, the power of the state may be eternal, but I cannot believe the same of any industrial firm. A person as uninformed as myself might well believe that a company would crumble if the profit motive disappeared. Yet, it now seems that big business, having already gone beyond that kind of innocent assumption, has established a means to continue its existence even if the state should disappear altogether. Shimada's words, which express the real feelings of a man who held a responsible position, are probably frank and genuine. But what is really supporting those feelings? He could certainly have disregarded the inevitable finger-pointing by making the excuse that "everybody gets mixed up in that kind of thing, somehow or other. . . ." Taking a harder look, I feel that lurking behind Shimada's word "eternal" lie the feelings of a man with a serious flaw; it seems that he had some desire to rescue himself through his suicide. His view of his firm as eternal certainly grew out of a sense of the commonality inherent in the idea of Family. He tried in death to latch on to the logic of the Family so as to pacify the company, public opinion, and finally himself. In other words, Shimada did not choose for himself a personal and quiet death, but sought to martyr himself for his master, as in the old feudal days.

Certainly, contemporary Japanese enterprise, full of such slogans as "Japan National Railway—One Family!" has produced corporate bodies that resemble "families" insofar as they follow the principles of group character. The purpose of forming such a group is clearly to seek profit, and they appear to follow the concepts inherent in the *iemoto* or Family Master system, but there are some fundamental differences as well. Despite the fact that no ties of blood are involved, emphasis is placed on the development of a community even stronger than blood, family, and fraternity. Various roles are assigned in a fixed hierarchy, to protect the autonomy of the group and to establish a community that cannot be interrupted, even by death. Various logics are developed, and individuals are urged to carry out spontaneous actions in support of the objectives of the group. In its collective aspect, at least, the modernization of Japan shows a history of adaptability to the group principle that is unique to this country.

Max Weber has pointed out that the ancestors of modern Western capitalism followed a principle of Protestant fru-

gality, and if a comparison can be made with the moderniz-
ing of Japan, I believe it would rest in the logic of the Family.
After all, *Shintō* [the most ancient of Japanese religions],
which spread among the people as a folk religion, consists
of a faith in the family, and latent within such a belief lies the
logic of an incentive to construct a larger society from such
elements. In this case, however, it must be noted that there
is a fundamental difference between Japan and the West in
the way in which the concept of God was first formulated in
terms of the configurations of religious faith.

Kamishima Jirō,
The Structure of Modern Japanese Thought

When I first read the newspaper articles about Shimada's
suicide I began to think of the *nō* actors, who have managed to
continue on into the modern world with the support of this faith
in the Family that comes all the way from *Shintō*. I thought of
how a *nō* actor might envision his own death on the stage. I remember thinking that, for all the individuality inherent in that
death, the situation would not now require him to reconfirm the
eternity of the group to which he belonged; nor would he think
of it as dying "on duty."

For us, the unnatural death of Shimada seems familiar, as it
confirms our sense of the smallness, the limits, of an individual
human being. True, one might not be able to imagine such conduct oneself, but the idea of a death of sacrifice for some
commonality is, in its psychological possibilities, something that
anyone who belongs to a group functioning in our system of contemporary capitalism can certainly imagine. How could it be,
then, that death among *nō* actors alone can be seen as natural,
exhibiting a dignity and a sense of peace? What allows for this?

Of course, as I mentioned earlier, *nō* actors possess such a
community of performance skills that even if the *shite* were to die
during the action, the play would continue. As the artistic space
is fixed, the movements are arranged in terms of a regulated envi-

ronment. Even the order of the dramas is completely determined; all individuality has been rendered altogether abstract.
The individual experiences of the actors and differences in their
levels of artistic accomplishment may exist, but they can never
emerge as factors inhibiting the development of the performer's
skills; certainly this is a danger in a modern theatre company.
Yet, no matter how homogeneous their methods of performance, the art of the *nō* actors is not one of mere animal reflex. A
nō performance cannot come into being without a harmony of
psychological movement as well. These actors are not soldiers;
and yet if one performer should fall dead before their eyes, the
group would show no change in the quality of its performance.
One wonders just how strong and how authentic their common
psychological effort can be, if this is the case.

Of course, I have never seen a *nō* actor expire before my eyes
on the stage; and if I had, certain doubts would have arisen at
once. Can you imagine that the actor's wife, sitting in the audience, could see her husband collapse and sit still right through to
the end of the performance? Or that a son perhaps, or a colleague in the chorus, would not call the performance to a halt?
Or that the members of the audience themselves, who had come
to see that particular actor perform, would simply sit and watch
the *kōken,* without a proper mask and costume, carry right
along? Would they not demand a refund? The fact is, these
reactions never take place. On the contrary, no matter how
"unartistic" the acting of the *kōken* might be, everyone in the *nō*
theatre, audience and players alike, are struck by the awesome
solemnity of such a moment. Even in the midst of our high-pow-
ered capitalist society, in the small-scale enterprise that
represents the world of art, this uniformity of response to the
death of a single man possesses something admirable about it,
and something uncanny as well. For one would have thought the
art world to be filled with people discontented over the exploita-
tion inherent in the *iemoto* system; to be engaged in many power
struggles and gloomy human relationships.

I have asked two or three *nō* actors the real significance of this whole matter. Their response is simply that, ever since they were children, they were told continually that even if a performer perished, nothing should be permitted to stop a performance. Such was the hereditary view, that was all. Probably in the medieval, feudal age, when the *nō* was first developed, the *nō* actors who performed before their patrons (the *Shōgun* or the *daimyō*) looked on their performances as a form of battle. If they lost their patrons' approbation, then the good name of their family would be destroyed and the company members would be turned out to fend for themselves as beggars. The idea of death, then, must have had great immediacy for them. For those actors, the situation must have very closely resembled that of a battle. If a military commander were to die, another would have to be chosen to replace him and lead the troops. Without such an attitude, the actors could not have appeared on the stage. This is related in turn to a belief among the actors that they began their trade as "beggars in a riverbed," giving rise to groundless prejudice against them. Mixed in as well, in some complex way, was a sense of self-contempt stemming from their conviction that they served in a kind of service industry. For such reasons, *nō* actors seem to have developed, as part of their aesthetic vocational ethic, the need to assume at all times this battle psychology on the stage.

Generally speaking, of course, there are many of us who would see the idea of dying on the job as a noble one. *Nō* actors have long made this attitude a common assumption, although in fact, the official adoption of such a code of behavior is a fairly recent phenomenon, one that probably originated in the late nineteenth century, sometime shortly after the Meiji Restoration in 1868. At the present time, the real grounding for such an attitude has already eroded, or at least become relative. It is certainly true that there would be no protest from an audience these days if such a performance were quickly terminated.

In the end, it is their remarkable heritage that permits *nō* actors to create gestures of true dignity and majesty, just as though they had no individual sense of their corporeal being, as though for them individuality represented only an abstract idea. Their ensemble seems actually to have created the kind of immortality that Mr. Shimada dreamt of. Whether or not one can speak of such a communality as the highest happiness that an individual can attain, of course, remains a moot point indeed.

One serious problem, then, concerning the concept of the Family, can be understood through an examination of this matter of the onstage death of a *nō* leading player.

3

Human Experience and the Group

Whatever the problems involved, every individual—regardless of his age, his sex—from his birth until his death, faces all issues on the level of personal experience. What interests me now is to discover in what form personal experiences can be incorporated into the structure of a group. National experience is woven from the commonality and diversity of all individual human experiences. To put it another way, what are the means by which the commonality of mankind's experiences can be passed on to the next generation? How is this process carried on? The contemporary means employed are radically different from those used in former times; in this regard, Japan has made a particularly strong break with the past in comparison with other cultures. Surely such problems as the cultural education of young people, the difficulties of aging, incidents of family violence, and the lack of any real international sense among contemporary Japanese people have arisen because of the means by which we transmit and deal with our sense of a common experience. Looking at specific cases involving the transmission of culture, various difficulties become apparent: problems with the organization of cultural and social groups as well as sexual differences, difficulties between children and parents, families, and so forth.

Because the theatre has always been a communal activity, the

[47]

problems of young versus old or men versus women are conceived of in contemporary and specific terms, and with an implicit and specific mandate to resolve them. For example, since the traditional Japanese performing arts are particularly involved with problems of youth and age, the theatre itself is conceived of in terms of such polarities, and the passing on of a commonality of vision must be ensured. Until the end of the war, there were many in the Japanese theatre who denied this traditional commonality altogether, branding the traditional art forms as feudal, premodern. Yet, examining the supposedly feudal period, an age that seems so different from our own, one actually finds an approach strikingly similar to ours toward the problems of age and youth revealed quite clearly in the traditional performing arts.

Traditional attitudes demand that respect be paid to the depth of human experience, the value of which can be determined by the extent to which those experiences are held in common. Such experiences extend beyond the spiritual occurrences shared by everyone. That is not to say that the regular course of a lived life—birth, childhood, youth, and the bodily changes that we experience as we grow weaker with old age—should merely be set aside. But in the world of the theatre in particular, the value of experience comes from determining how changes in age and body can be put to use. Relevant experience must be developed by the actors through their own self-consciousness of those changes. Therefore, the talents of a mature performer are naturally more fully developed than those of a youthful actor. An old actor, by drawing on his objective sense of the richness of his own personal human experience, can reach the fullest flowering of his talent. Human experience, then, requires development over an extended period of time. This attitude is most prevalent in the *nō* theatre, in which it continues to be assumed that artistic possibilities increase as an actor grows older. In the *nō*, an actor of about twenty may well be praised for his youthful sensibilities—what Zeami called "the young blossom." But he must also come to realize that he will grow older in terms of his physical means of expression. What then becomes most important is the way in which he takes control of these changes, and the manner in which he deals with them. The strength of his art comes from the value he places on the skills developed in his own body. From this point of view, an actor's skills develop fully only in his older age. So it is entirely reasonable that the older actor, who has completed the process of physical and psychological change, will naturally lead a privileged existence in the midst of his troupe.

In the traditional performing arts, and particularly in the *nō,* such considerations have always been particularly clear. The *nō* stage, for example, is the one place where all of the beauty and richness of human experience are given focus, and the changes brought about by human experience are made palpable, through the troupe's skill in representing mankind's commonality. To a certain extent, the attitudes embodied on stage can be considered representative of the feudal past; still, it seems altogether natural that a *nō* or *kabuki* actor can only become the Real Thing as he grows older.

It is certainly true that, however apprehensive a young *nō* actor may feel as he walks out onto the bridge that leads to the stage, the same movement will come to seem simpler as he grows older. His body will eventually come to feel a greater freedom as he continues to respond to his particular environment. Such is human nature that, given an environment riddled with restrictive conventions, a man feels freer as he gains in experience—that is, as he grows older. Older *kabuki* and *nō* actors, in their freedom, thus appear remarkably animated. Although they may experience some waning of physical strength, their spirits appear young and fresh. This youthfulness can be said to arise from a sense of freedom within restriction, as well as a consciousness of that freedom.

Because a young actor has not had much experience, his body has little sense of freedom, and he thus may sense a feeling of oppression. Assigned to perform a series of restricted move-ments, he cannot quickly internalize them, master them. Those physical restrictions thus represent a form of oppression for young actors against which they must struggle. The struggle may continue on without their being conscious of the process; or per-haps they feel that they can win the battle. In any case, they remain captives of the situation, they are not free, they constrain themselves. When this kind of fighting energy is felt in the act-ing, it creates in the audience a sense of restrictiveness, of disquiet.

When the transition from one generation to another takes place as a natural process in the traditional performing arts, the connections between those restrictions and conventions, when involved in a traditional sense of commonality, function in terms of an organizational psychology. However, should the substance of the system collapse, then such a way of life, the kind of spiritual and physical devices that were created in response to fixed conditions and restrictions, will be turned upside down in terms of the structural relationships, inevitably political, be-tween the controller and the controlled. They will be improperly used.

On the other hand, many young people who have gone to study in Europe wish to abandon any such communal control, and are quick to point out and condemn the existence of such structures. It was out of just such rebellion, of course, that the idea of a modern theatre in Japan was born. It seems to me that the major battle of the Japanese theatre in our century, a struggle involving both the traditional and the modern theatre, has fo-cused and must continue to focus on the vital matter of how to establish a useful connection between the natural process of ag-ing and the universality of human experience. The struggle also involves deciding which aspect of the relationship should receive the emphasis. The choice, conscious or unconscious, of where to place that emphasis vitally affects the very concept of the theatre that is created. Such assumptions have affected the kind of stage to be used, the role of the director, and the style of acting. In the end, the modern theatre movement in Japan has been Romantic in nature, and so has valued the outpouring of youthful individuality, the potential flowering from within the individual.

As I suggested above, in the classical performing arts, the idea remains that as an actor grows older, his personal experience, gained in the context of a set of restrictions, comes into play. The actor undergoes various experiences so that eventually he achieves a kind of communal self-consciousness (another term, if you like, for artistic freedom). The kind of freedom to which he aspired when he was young can only truly be achieved as the body ages. Thus, all the restrictions he faces serve as a kind of lengthy initiation ceremony. This is, in its way, a truly admirable aesthetic, of which *nō* actors should be very proud.

If one looks at the various theatrical devices employed in the *nō*—the use of the stage, the various fixed patterns of performance, the use of hereditary professional names—it may seem on the surface that distinctions between young and old performers are maintained. In fact, however, such distinctions simply do not apply; rather, the distinction maintained in the ensemble is between performers who are free and those who are not.

The initiation I mentioned above does not function to separate adults from children. Rather, there is an assumption as to the relative profundity of an actor's experience in relation to the communal experience; this distinction is really no more than a code of behavior affirmed by all. The level of deliberately created communality has no reason to depend, then, on distinctions between youth and age, adults and children. To put it another way, in this system children are conceived of only as small adults. The essence of the matter lies in the creation of a communal sense of what individuals have lived through, what has come to be called "experience." What is at stake is the depth of that experience. It is not a question of merely dividing humans by a quantitative standard of choronology, of age. In terms of performance, the piling up of years does not automatically convey artistic adulthood; only the depth of experience through which the actor has lived in the troupe is of value.

The contemporary system of conveying adulthood in society through an educational system is exemplified by the student who spends six years in primary school and then has adulthood automatically conferred at twenty. His status is decided from the outside on the basis of a homogeneity of experience, so that respect is automatically earned with age. This view seems in absolute contrast to the older system, wherein a young actor, even a child actor, if skillful in ensemble, could be considered an adult if he helped give life to the experience of the group. He would thus be considered a full-fledged participant. Unfortunately, modern education has merely formalized the process it proposed to create. Those who do not attend primary school are considered to have achieved nothing, yet no one asks what those six years of training may have consisted of. If real human differences were taken into account, then surely there would be those who could graduate, say, in four years. The decision would be based on each individual's personal life history, it seems to me, rather than on issues of relative skill.

In recent times, the concept of experience has come to be measured by the calendar time involved. Modern ideas of education presume that if experience can be measured in terms of time, then, after a certain number of years have gone by, various skills will inevitably have been mastered. Such is not held to be the case in the traditional performing arts, where even a young performer is assumed to possess an intuitive sense of the relation between his age and his experience. A child actor of ten may one day create a moment of incredible depth in his performance, while another may lose his talent by the time he is twenty. The same ten-year-old, performing some particular part, may give the impression that he is thirty, even forty. It is a system of restrictions that makes such accomplishments possible.

Suppose, for example, an extraordinarily precocious performer of twenty appears. His talent surely arises from his family situation, from the nature of the human relationships in which he has been involved. Another, because of his family upbringing, may know nothing. The difference between them has nothing to do with their relative ages; it arises from their personal life experiences.

Although not all aspects of ordinary life were so tightly regulated up until the modern period, the positive aspects of these older ways of thinking did make themselves felt in the area of the traditional performing arts. From a contemporary vantage point outside the system, such attitudes may appear formalistic and quantitative, but I believe there were actually considerations of quality involved as well. In the modern period, however, quantitative considerations have come into importance. The concept of time now dominates, making questions of youth and age very important.

As I mentioned above, a freedom from the distinctions between youth and age based on the linear passage of time is attained in the traditional performing arts through a process of initiation that does away with time as a series of linear moments. The preservation of this artistic reality has been achieved through the use of fixed patterns of performance. These fixed forms of ensemble performance provide a means to prove the communality of the experience involved: if patterns can exist, then there must lie behind them a genuine spirit of the group. Therefore, the fundamental structure of a traditional arts ensemble is not based on individuals; rather, its assets accrue from the wisdom passed on by the group, the vision created from the communal experience of a whole family of actors. In our century, those "families" are no longer created by ties of blood but are based on the economic necessities of performance, without considerations of any spiritual bond. Nevertheless, those families have created a particular approach to performance. A close examination of that approach employed by an ensemble makes it possible to understand at once whether a young actor is able to match his experience to that of the group. In order to transcend questions of age, in fact, the concept of chronological age is dispensed with by using such strategies as casting a hitherto minor actor in an important role, or granting the family name to a young actor not necessarily related by blood.

But then, as in all human affairs, difficulties appear. Zeami, in speaking of artistic succession by family, insisted that true succession does not derive strictly from bloodlines. For him, the creation of a true "House" was possible only through an inheritance based on the quality of the group's experience. He meant that art survives with the help of this device. By now, the concept of selective succession has degenerated into an economic system of pyramidal hierarchy, the *iemoto,* or tradition of the Master Teacher. But we should not forget that Zeami and his father Kan'ami understood the paramount importance of maintaining a truly communal approach. They were convinced that a troupe could only continue on under the leadership of the actor who had best mastered this communal method, regardless of his age or bloodlines.

People in modern theatre refuse to regard the matter of succession in the traditional theatre as Zeami envisioned it; rather, they look on the *iemoto* system as a mere commercial framework based on bloodline. And they think they must invent a new sort of commonality for their theatre troupes. The consciousness, the feelings that support such attitudes, represent a contemporary criticism of the traditional performing arts that, interestingly enough, is not far in spirit from the doubts expressed by Zeami. New standards have now appeared for judging a group, based on ideology and conceptual theatre. Does not a commonality of ideas create a collectivity without regard for age, sex, or other distinctions among the actors? It is ideas that should resolve differences that arise within the group, ideas that set courses of action, and ideas should provide the group with its *raison d'être.* Or so their proponents believe, in any case.

These days, excuses disguised as ideology are invoked when a drama company is dissolved. None of the real reasons—"I can't get along with the troupe;" "I can't deal with the culture of the young;" "you're too old and I don't want to work with you any more"—are articulated. Even when the reasons are emotional—the real generation gap, the problems of older directors and younger actors getting along—those who quit always say, "I can no longer agree with the principles on which the troupe is being run. So I resign."

Up until my generation, all theatre people described their actions in this fashion, as if ideological warfare were the definitive manifestation of their real feelings. Presumably, all those who belonged to groups motivated by politics behaved like that. Everything was put forth as a matter of principle. The front they put on and their ulterior motives differed considerably, however.

Trouble over the ages of actors and the difficulties between actors and actresses seem most likely to erupt in modern theatre troupes. Presumably this is because there exists an unarticulated assumption that the difficulties arising from such distinctions should not be expressed openly. It is difficult to understand how such beliefs have become implanted, yet they now appear somehow fundamental. Perhaps a kind of modern humanism has brought them into being. In any case, theatre people talk on and on, insisting that good human relations must be established for the benefit of communication and a communal vision. Yet they insist that no distinctions of sex or age should enter into forming such a communal vision, particularly in a group conscious of its real artistic identity. The same belief is held by those who organize theatrical groups along political lines.

Yet when any such communal principles are actually put into practice, there follows a rejection of any succession of bloodlines or families, and so no means are provided by which a group dedicated to a certain set of ideas can assure its continuity. Before the modern period, when it came to such matters as social position or the differences between the roles of men and women, all groups were strongly molded by societal forces. Pushed into such preordained forms, the members found it fairly easy to pass along their communal vision.

In recent times, the well-known, politically progressive actor Uno Jūkichi has put forth a "theory of a sole generation" as appropriate for a modern theatre troupe. Yet if only one generation exists, then no one feels the need to pass on his or her experiences. There is no motivation to develop any scheme beyond oneself in order to carry an idea further. Such attitudes have caused a real rupture between the generations. All considerations center on what one has done oneself, *oneself;* there seems to be no thought of devising a plan for passing on experience to the next generation.

Why is Uno content to contemplate the work of one generation alone? It must be remembered that any modern theatre troupe that seeks to reproduce itself must have been constructed in terms of modern ideas of independence and equality in the first place. The establishment of any special relationships that might be seen as "feudal" will be obvious at once. Modern theatre people will condemn these attitudes and see them as revealing a lack of modern consciousness.

Since individual skills cannot be passed on to the next generation, then what about artistic experience? Those in charge are more or less forced into accepting the principles of a one-generation artistic effort. There seems to them something pure and righteous about such a quick dissolution, and there remains a romantic Japanese quality in such an attitude. Of course this does not apply to those groups that seek only profit. Modern theatre troupes founded on artistic principles, holding the basic attitude that through artistic skill, imperfect human relationships can somehow be rendered spiritually rich, are driven to the conscientious conclusion that their troupes ought to cease to exist after one generation.

One would suppose then, that those men and women wishing to form a group based on modern perceptions of human relationships must be ready to weary themselves with the problems of evaluating their experience so as to continue their efforts, and then to identify the means to ensure succession for a meaningful period of time. But on the other hand, such concerns seem to cause them to feel that they are somehow conservative, even reactionary, but certainly not truly modern. They may feel intimidated by such matters. Since modern troupes see no value in turning theatrical experience into communal succession, it follows that the stream of present-day Japanese theatre troupes represents the culture of youth: they have broken with the troupes that preceded them. And since those older troupes have only thought of their work in terms of one generation as well, they too are incapable of bringing forward something new. Their members can only grow old together as a group. When something new appears, they can find no way to make use of it; they see it as something outside themselves, only an "exception." Such is the situation in which the modern theatre troupes in Japan find themselves, it seems to me.

My own purpose is to create a kind of work unrelated to matters of age or gender. Who wouldn't strive to develop a theatrical conception capable of transcending such distinctions? Yet we live at a time when the tendency toward a rupture between the generations is pronounced, when a youth culture is strong, when things are not going smoothly. Any effort to establish communication through the sharing of individual experiences seems to have disappeared; only an externalized communality, based on the fleeting popularity of something on television or on some best-seller or other, seems to exist.

What is missing is the healthy sort of communication that develops when we have had the opportunity, based on our ages and life histories, to consider the depths of our own personal experiences, both in their unique and their common aspects. Joint experience, after all, begins with a consciousness of personal experience; one compares one's own development with that of others, examines the differences and locates the common factors, which may include the kinds of connections one has with one's family, what one has read, and so forth. These various life experiences can then be objectified in terms of mutuality, so that a genuine communication can begin to develop. Such issues as the status of the sexes and the differences between the generations will form a part of this communality; but in order for a group to develop in this fashion, it must resist the hard, monolithic surfaces in favor of a many-sided, open vision.

In the actual conduct of contemporary Japanese theatre companies, the biggest problem today seems to involve a lack of an *appropriate* standard of dedication. For example, an actor in rehearsal may suddenly announce, "My mother's coming up to town today, so I have to pass up this practice. I'll be leaving now." This kind of behavior is not "up to standard," and what is more, the whole idea of a "standard" that could even consider condoning such an attitude is highly suspect. To speculate on this kind of behavior further, let us assume that the person who asked for time off knew from the beginning that the request was inappropriate, but just wanted to check to see how far he could go. What are the standards he is "checking" against? This kind of problem arises in managing an established company on a day-to-day basis which is maintained on the principle of joint experience.

If a group is not being run for profit, if its communality is based not on economics but on the purity of a common response to a set of theories, then how can its idealism hold up in actual practice? When personal "space" is permitted to intrude on the vision of the group, there will be real difficulty in attempting to regulate the problems that will inevitably arise. For example, every aspect of the terrorist group known as the Japanese Red Army is evidently centralized. In such a communal mode of thinking, the communality supports the collective vision in its entirety, and therefore, personal and everyday dimensions of living are fulfilled by the group. When a group, be it theatrical or political, establishes its own logic, the individual constituents of the group are forced to regard themselves only in terms of this framework. The fundamental inadequacy of such communal absolutism has by now been soundly proven.

How can these sorts of problems be resolved in the climate of our society today? The usual answer is to "talk them over," which may appear to be the only means available to resolve any differences. And how can the problems be resolved so that the situation will settle down? In the end, all that will be said is that "the actor is still immature," or, "you can't trust young people these days," or, "his education at home was bad." The grumbling goes on, but finally, the personal selfishness of the actor has to be accepted. In the end, I feel, no real standards are ever upheld.

These difficulties arise in every sort of situation, and when the ensemble spirit of a theatre troupe is in jeopardy, they occur all the more often. Of course, a new member of the company cannot have had the benefit of the communal experience of the group, and his difficulties will be that much greater if he has had no previous theatre experience. For that reason, a process of education, of initiation, becomes necessary. There must be sessions impressing such newcomers with the fact that the troupe operates as it does because of the vision that all its members possess in common, a vision based on the experiences of the troupe. Those, therefore, who deviate from such ideals, or who attempt to disrupt that vision, will be regarded as a threat to the livelihood of the troupe and can expect to be ostracized. But such punishment is impossible in the world of today's theatre, for although the troupe does earn its living together, individual participants join on the basis of their own subjective motivations. A free and open group would thus not, in principle, seek to apply constraints that were too stringent; they could not, in fact, expect to impose themselves on an individual in this fashion. All too often, the result is that the logic of the troupe dissolves; there remain no means to resolve differences on other than an individual and subjective basis. A communal vision or set of ideas cannot thrive in such an atmosphere; and in the case of a clash, the level of discourse leading to a solution is immediately lowered to the realm of personal feelings. In another sense, all the possible means of enforcing standards are reduced to a matter of preference: "I like it" or "I don't." The theatre companies in Japan maintain their dedication to a special vision which they stoutly maintain they will realize, but none can show that they have actually developed a system that will be able to continue on into the future. They have found no clear means to pass along their experiences. And there is seemingly no way to educate them to do so. There seems, therefore, no way to "check up on" the private behavior of each individual member of the troupe.

In my view, the most important work of a theatre troupe does not involve any simple spreading about of its message, whatever that may be. The group must instead take charge of expressing a felt responsibility for finding a means to pass along the unique experiences that the group has undergone. This is because, in practical terms, individual judgments can and must be questioned. However, as I mentioned above, since the theatre involves an expression of the relations among living human beings, it is quite possible that the methods chosen to communicate experiences will reveal elements of an older thinking mixed in with them. After all, Japan maintains a number of premodern attitudes; contemporary human relations still reveal certain feudal aspects. Because of this, often no attempt is made actually to explicate any methods developed by a group. Until now, no troupe has as yet thought through the issues to this extent. This is doubtless why Uno Jūkichi mandates that the lifespan of a theatre be confined to one sole generation.

According to a newspaper report, the famous modern playwright Kinoshita Junji has said that he does not wish his most popular play, *Yūzuru* (*Evening Crane*), staged without the actress Yamamoto Yasue, for whom he wrote the play originally and who has performed the role so often. Yet, what about the actors who have worked under Uno or Yamamoto? These performers have been able to do what they have done precisely because of the ensemble to which they belong; yet, the fact that the troupe will disband at Uno's retirement (or at Yamamoto's death) would seem to indicate that the scope of the communal experience must be identified with a particular generation or individual. Of course, in one sense the feelings of such a crucial performer are credible enough. In a way, Uno's attitude reveals a commendable fastidiousness. Yet there is another way to see the issue, one that focuses instead on the regularization of the activities of the group, one that insists that the communal experience should be made visible in the troupe's public performances. Based on those sorts of assumptions, Uno's attitude seems unfortunate, excessively individualistic, even somewhat Romantic. There seems something peculiar about the leader of a troupe who announces beforehand that only one generation of performances can be sustained. Of course, if a troupe achieves no success, it will have to disband whether its members wish to establish a second generation or not. But if the leader is to decide that the group will be disbanded in a generation, he would have been better off not beginning his efforts in the first place. No group can be reduced to a single individual.

Theatre people exist in a day-to-day relationship to their troupe; they carry on their work based on the assumption that if the others did not exist, they could not exist either. For this reason, it is highly important that each individual have the strength to pass on what he has experienced. Of course, each period in history creates its own climate of ideas; and within the troupe itself, differences of opinion will persist based on disparities in age and sex. All of these relationships, in fact, can become quite complicated. But when a performer strives to pass along what he has done, and seeks to find a suitable means to express his experiences, then, must not those who direct the troupe provide the means? *Kabuki* and other traditional performing arts possess such means of expression. Whether or not an individual performer can fully grasp those means is beside the point. The *iemoto* system provides a method by which the secret of the art is transferred from father to son, so that the chief actor can say, "this is the way I want to pass on my experience;" "this is how a *nō* stage should be constructed and used by future generations;" "this is how I would like a lifetime of practical experience to be understood."

These days, however, other attitudes prevail in the contemporary theatre. Some take the view that one generation is enough; some put a premium on expressing a particular set of emotional responses, assuming that their will in such matters will simply be heeded by their companies. People who hold these views plan for a literary and not a theatrical succession, for it is their ideas and not any theatrical techniques that they wish to transmit. Yet what is really important to pass along are the new means of expression that the actors can learn as a group, the specific techniques. For it is precisely when a troupe is at the point of devising the techniques to pass along new experiences that it is able to throw some light on the real nature of the difficulties inherent in the areas of contemporary thought and social behavior alike.

The process of inheritance or transmission need not involve any forcing of experience. The desire to impart the significance and the reality of human experience, from birth to death, is a fundamental one. Mankind exists; each individual exists alone; the pain of such an existence, the sadness of it, and of course the joy of it as well, must all be conveyed. One way to do so is through the theatre. It is to promote such communication that men and women of the theatre must work, as they construct their troupes toward an artistic end. And they must come to terms with the problem of how to devise techniques to promote this communication; to avoid the issue would be tantamount to confessing one's defeat in the face of the old feudalistic system of behavior and succession. That would certainly be inconsistent with the aims of modern theatre, which sets out—in revolt against the traditional theatre—to create a truly contemporary, communal artform.

I would say in criticism of the modern theatre movement in Japan that it exhibits virtually no inclination toward any methods truly appropriate to the *theatre* as an artform. Proper methods would not seek to stop at the level of individual memory; they would attempt to render individual memory universal, and on a scale consonant with a theatrical ensemble. At best, ideals of performance should be developed into a practical system; and even if that level cannot be reached, there is certainly no reason to give up trying, and so reveal a total lack of any critical spirit whatsoever.

No one among modern theatre people ("modernists," they might be termed) shows any such intentions. None of these modernists or political progressives can proclaim with dignity that they have found a new means to transmit their experiences, or that they are seeking a method that differs from those still enmeshed in old feudal attitudes. In fact, they only encourage the very sort of re-feudalization that they are at pains to criticize. This tendency in the contemporary theatrical world stems from a lack of confidence in the transmission of experience. Artists, in a mood of defeatism, want to abandon the search altogether, to settle merely for making money, to allow the *iemoto* system to stand as it is, to abandon any real standards.

If I may express my opinion as a man of the theatre, I feel that if the members of a group truly wish to seek a means to transmit their art—a group not out for money, nor one with some pronounced political view, but a troupe with a true communal vision to express—they can, if they take up the challenge in a conscious manner, clarify the difficulties facing our society in general, the disparities between the sexes and generations. I would even submit that theatre people are especially qualified for the task.

It seems to me that the fundamental problems of society at large are in fact closely intertwined with matters of communality and the transmission of the theatrical experiences of a group. Someone, someday, will find a means to surmount the obstacles

of age and sex inherent in the structures of our theatre companies. He who tries faces an enormous task and many continuing
setbacks. Yet such an attempt is crucial in order to ensure the
future of the contemporary theatre.

Problems in society at large reveal themselves in various ways:
a revival of fundamentalist religion, the rise of the Japanese Red
Army, violence in the home. What is more, the fundamental
issues at stake for society are not always evident from each separate manifestation or example. Some issues, of course, arise of
their own accord, and it seems that no larger, more basic
problem can be extracted from them; it might be said that no
existing group possesses the means to extract a larger meaning
from a given incident.

How can the fundamental issues of age and sex be understood, articulated, put in order? Only, it seems to me, when a
group is formed that can comprehend how such problems can be
transcended, molded into a communality and in turn passed
along to future generations.

The time has come when disparities based on age and sex are
beginning to disappear. Despite inevitable differences in age and
body structure, such distinctions seem to be emphasized less and
less in the conduct of daily life. And I doubt if they will return to
the fore. Whatever happens, whether women become asexual,
homosexuality spreads, nineteen-year-old women take to marrying sixty-year-old men or free sex becomes the norm (and I make
no judgments here of any kind), any shifts in the social system
will doubtless come about naturally, as a matter of course. But
whatever happens, one thing is clear: the basic distinctions between sex and age will continue to remain altogether apparent and visible. However they may be glossed over, I don't think
that any attempt can ever be made to suppress their existence
entirely.

What should be realized is that, against the tide of the age, some artifical, unnatural ways of thinking must deliberately be employed in an attempt to recognize anew, and then suppress, those necessary distinctions. Various methods of de-emphasizing them have been attempted in earlier periods of history, and indeed, some of those patterns of thought actually took on functional significance. But aspects of the old methods have lost effectiveness as old systems have given way. Appropriate new methods require new words, new perceptions. Yet, how few efforts are being made to discover them. The whole issue may have to be forgotten, or simply looked upon as some sentimental relic.

A theatre troupe that rejects the family model and seeks to perpetuate itself through the individual development of its members can today only hope for change through sentimental and emotional factors. Groups that center on ideas will in the end be destroyed, since the moment must come when their ethics can no longer be trusted. At that point, each time an issue comes up, the response to it must be based entirely on the individual's emotional state—"do I like it or not?" The general level of ethical thinking thus ultimately drops to the level of individual preference. Society is indeed shot through with protestantism! The highest standard of ethics no longer consists of a belief in the truth shared with others. The situation has become very serious.

I am convinced that ethics can only play a part in human relationships if man believes in a universality outside himself. These days, however, little concern is shown for the truth expressed by another. The very concept of an objective truth itself does not develop. Truth has come to be regarded as a kind of deception. And because human relationships are now conceptualized in terms of psychology, *anomie* has become a reality. In this environment, individual distinctions of sex and age have now become all the more strikingly evident. The old now merely see themselves as old, and feel an obsessive inferiority to the young. The young are merely young, and nervous about their difficulties in communicating with their elders. When people meet on the level of "male" and "female," men bring an entire complex of sexual feelings to their dealings with women. Thus, while distinctions in the social system seem to be breaking down, the real differences are becoming all the more obvious. All of these distinctions now manifest themselves in physiological ways, spontaneously, even on our very faces.

In such circumstances, when thinking about the formation of a theatre group, the only possibility may seem to be to put things together on the basis of likes and dislikes, on a foundation of sentimentality. That seems to me to sum up the problems encountered in attempting to work together.

The kind of troupe I envision would not come into being along those lines. The emotional bond I seek would not be that of some Nazi-like group. Such devotion to a group can only, after a time, give rise to an emperor, a dictator. The vital element should be not a sense of devotion itself, but the manifestation of another quality, one that grows out of that devotion, a sense that there is a certain level of regulation necessary for the sake of the group, a sense of the need for rules and prescribed ways to pass on experiences. Of course, all this can be carried out in a frivolous spirit; I am afraid that today, in fact, there sadly remain only two impulses in the theatre—one, a determination to be frivolous, and the other, a desire to make rules.

Yet, if the initial energy involved consists not in the emotion itself but in a belief in the importance of emotional attachment, then perhaps the individual can indeed come to feel that the emotions of the others are genuine as well. Thus, he will begin to examine his own personal experience in order to determine what he holds in common with the others, and learn how that understanding can be passed along. A life could be spent in finding these answers. The matter of human existence raises a series of crucial questions: how can those who differ in age and sex truly build a means of communication with one another, one that is based on a real sense of mutual affection? And on what scale can this be accomplished? Can a means of communication be established that transcends the differences between men and women? The seeking out of the means to this end must continue if the real differences that divide us are ever to be surmounted, so that human existence can come to mean the same for everyone.

There are those who regard the characteristics of a theatre troupe to be akin to those of a religious cult—a People's Temple. There is, of course, no similarity whatsoever. After all, the activities engaged in by a political or religious group do not have to be exhibited openly; exposure does not constitute the fundamental reason for its existence. On the other hand, a theatre group, which gains its sense of authenticity only from what others see in it, must expose itself to the public. Its primary goal is to be seen. The premise is that the success or failure of what a company shows to the public is crucial. Theatre troupes are often criticized for taking on mystical overtones or closing themselves off completely. It would be a misconception to operate a troupe on any such principles. No troupe could continue its activities based on such ideas: it would dissolve of its own accord. Indeed, the opposite tendency is more likely to exist: a troupe will simply retreat into commercialism, into pleasing its customers, and so abandon any critical examination of its own purposes. A theatre troupe, by definition, is not complete within itself. That is why old actors in the traditional performing arts continue to be considered "young."

In any theatre group, those who hold one set of assumptions can band together so as to impose their own experience on the others for verification. When such a group is able to function, it wields considerable power, and those who join in can retain their youth. The very word "group" seems to suggest, erroneously, a sense of communal closure. Certainly in the case of the "Ark of Jesus," a celebrated religious group active in Japan in the 1970s, the members cut themselves off in a manner that suggested a real flight from society. In the case of the People's Temple, its members went all the way to Guyana. In groups like these, such developments are logical; the members have nothing to show to others, no reason to come into contact with any criticism from outside.

Therefore, when a theatre troupe is assembled on the basis of some artifical principle, the problem is the level of artificiality. No matter how small such a troupe may be, if it is formed to exist entirely within itself, there can be no effective communication possible with other groups. It has only been since the 1960s, in fact, that troupes in Japan have striven to achieve a more universal status, dedicated from the first to communication, rather than to maintaining some sort of exclusivity. It is for this reason, I think, that scholastic as well as other kinds of artistic activities have drawn closer to the theatre, and that various dialogues have come to take place between those various artforms. In simplest terms, the theatre is a transmission of the forms of human action. These actions are no special property of the theatre; rather, the theatre functions as a model for the whole cultural mechanism, and how we must deal with our communal experiences. No wonder people from various intellectual disciplines are more and more attracted by the vision that the theatre—as a movement— can encompass.

4

The Toga Festival

My Experience in France

My first occasion to go abroad was about ten years ago. I was invited by the consummate French director Jean-Louis Barrault to participate in the international festival held at the Théâtre des Nations in Paris. In the Japanese delegation were Shiraishi Kayoko and myself, the great *nō* actor Kanze Hisao, now deceased, his younger brother Kanze Hideo, the celebrated *kyōgen* performer Nomura Mansaku, and Watanabe Moriaki, a professor of French from Tokyo University. Our delegation had been assigned the topic, "The Theatre and Body Movement," with the idea that we might be able to present something on the theme of gesture and motion. We had decided to try a number of demonstrations. Kanze Hisao was to perform sections from the *nō* play *Dōjōji* (*Dōjō Temple*), Nomura Mansaku scenes from the *kyōgen* play *Tsurigitsune* (*Fox Trapping*), and Shiraishi was going to demonstrate our definition of the "theatrical."

The theatre in which we were to perform was used by Barrault's company and was then called the Théâtre Recamier. I had a number of remarkable surprises there.

For those in the Japanese theatrical world, and particularly for those in the generation ahead of me, Barrault was regarded as a kind of god among directors. He was exceedingly famous, so I imagined that his theatre would provide sumptuous surroundings. I was shocked to find it extremely sober and simple. And what is more, the performing space had been constructed in a surprising way. There was a special area made from several square rooms that must have once been used as living quarters. In the middle of this space an unusual stage had been built, with steps leading up to an elevated platform on all four sides. This atmosphere, austere, perhaps a bit peculiar, was used for all of the various presentations in the festival.

Since Paris is an international center, there was a huge audience interested in seeing all the productions. Arabs, Indians, Chinese, spectators from every country packed themselves in. Cultural officials and diplomats turned up as well. Drinks were served in the lobby, so when a performance was finished, people had a chance to talk quite easily about what they had seen, and in a very relaxed atmosphere. As the theatre was housed in what had been someone's home, the greenroom and even Barrault's dressing room were poor and cramped. Neither lighting nor sound equipment was fully satisfactory, and spare electronic parts were piled in a box, so that everyone felt his ingenuity well taxed. Despite alterations, remnants of the taste and thinking of the building's previous owners were in evidence, so that it seemed more like a reused residence than a theatre.

Seeing a number of performances there changed profoundly my idea of what the theatre could be.

In the first place, the theatre is not a fixed form to which an audience has a predetermined response. At Barrault's theatre everyone worked closely together to create the productions—directors, lighting technicians, property men, and scene shifters alike. For them and for the audience as well, the performance was a collective experience. The shared time called for inspiration from all who participated; the experience of the theatrical event convinced all of the participants that they had been part of a dramatic happening. They arrived at a sense of the theatrical experience freely, without any preconceptions of what that experience should be like.

As Japanese people, we have the image in our minds that the *nō* is to be performed on a properly designed *nō* stage. The nature of that stage is fixed: it has four pillars, a bridge, a wooden back wall with the traditional pine tree design, and musicians seated in front. The word *nō* immediately suggests such a fixed scene. As presented in Paris, however, *nō* gave an altogether different impression. When Kanze Hisao and his brother put on *Dōjōji,* the crowds swelled around the stage, more and more people pouring in until they had crowded right up to the raised stage itself, so that the playing space was narrowed considerably.

As presented in this fashion, *nō* revealed a strength it never exhibits in Japan, and I remember how deeply moved I was by what I saw. Surrounded by spectators, Hisao, in his mask and costume, performed the final scene with all his might, to thunderous applause. In the midst of his huge audience, sitting, crouching, sprawling, witnessed by Frenchmen, Chinese, and Indians, this *nō* actor matched his voice to the rhythms of the music as he played on through the voices thundering their appreciation. I became conscious all over again of both the mystery and the force of the *nō.*

As I said, we in Japan have a fixed image of the *nō.* In these terms, what I saw on that small stage in Paris, where even the actor's movements had to be modified, might not seem to constitute the real thing. I had always seen *nō* performed in the traditional way; now, watching a performance under these unusual circumstances, I was made to recognize its superb theatricality. The rigorous training that had tempered and shaped the body of the actor produced a brilliant liveliness on the stage, right down to the tiniest details of movement. The masks and costumes I knew so well sparkled in a new light. *Nō* in Paris was superb; the spectators were bewitched. For the first time I began to realize what Zeami meant when he spoke of *yūgen,* of stillness in a performance, or of the vision beyond sight. What I saw gave me enormous motivation. For me, this performance revealed more of the true spirit of the *nō* than performances given under orthodox conditions in a *nō* theatre, conditions that would normally be thought of as necessary.

Not just any *nō* actor, of course, could have accomplished this feat. The success of Kanze Hisao was contingent on his great abilities. Another performance given outside of the usual surroundings would not necessarily show off the *nō* in a proper light. In fact, such experiments undertaken by lesser artists would be likely to fail. But the experience at the Festival demonstrated that following the rules is not the only way to ensure a great performance. When a tradition can be successfully broken, the profundities of the *nō* can become all the more apparent.

I had always taken it for granted that actors performed in a designated playing space while the spectators sat and watched. After my experience at Barrault's theatre, I was bombarded with new ideas. On one occasion, the audience seemed to find a play staged by an English company boring; in the middle of the performance the cry went up, "Get off the stage! Off the stage!" The political relations between France and England are complicated, but politics did not inspire this outburst. The idea of the play seemed interesting, but in performance it lost its attraction, which annoyed the French spectators and caused the uproar. I was struck by the fact that the English actors responded vehemently, talking back to the audience; the whole theatre burst into sound and the play was interrupted time after time. Barrault then appeared and asked the spectators to watch for a bit longer. The actors began again but were halted five minutes later by more shouts of criticism. A feverish atmosphere continued to hang over the hall.

My experiences in France were very powerful ones, and upon returning to Japan, I harbored the dream of building a theatre similar to Barrault's.

I wanted, first of all, to throw out any preconceived notion of what a theatre should be. But I didn't want to replace it with some flashy new concept, the sort that might be created by an architect. I dreamt of making use of a space in which people had actually lived, a space filled with a history of actual human use. Wouldn't this be, I thought, the right environment for a truly contemporary theatre?

It seemed to me that in terms of traditional Japanese styles of architecture, there were only three possibilities that could provide the proper conditions: a castle, a Buddhist temple, or a mountain farmhouse, particularly the kind with a steeply pitched roof.

In Europe and America most buildings are made of stone, so that if walls and partitions are removed large spaces can be created. The ceilings are high, too. In the case of most Japanese buildings, however, the space between the pillars is narrow and the ceilings are low, which creates problems. Modern city dwellings in particular have low ceilings and small rooms. Only the three styles I chose seemed to avoid these difficulties. I knew that I could neither rent nor borrow a temple or castle, which left only the possibility of using a farmhouse for a theatre.

When I had reached this stage in my thinking, I learned that it might be possible to borrow a suitable house at Toga-mura. Not wanting to pass up such a chance, I paid a visit to the village. I remember the day very well. It was February 12, 1976. The place was buried deep in heavy snow, and the drifts were blowing badly. There were five old farmhouses there which had been moved and were no longer in use. I made arrangements on the spot to borrow one of them.

The farmhouse had precisely the right characteristics for a theatre. In the middle of the structure were six wooden pillars, and around a central "kitchen" were smaller rooms front and back, right and left. By putting the stage in the middle of the "kitchen," the pillars, being rather thick, gave the space at first glance the appearance of a *nō* stage. The pillars were about eighteen feet apart; but with the spacing rearranged, the distances between them could be enlarged to over twenty feet, so that the effect was indeed like a *nō* stage. Although, structurally speaking, these pillars were rather troublesome, they seemed fairly easy to move. (Five years later my friend Isozaki Arata and I would remove them and build our present stage.) This is how a mountain home for the Waseda Little Theatre came into being. (Mr. Isozaki, by the way, has designed a modern museum for the city of Los Angeles, and, with the support of the Governor of Toyama Prefecture, has also designed for us a new open-air theatre at the request of the villagers at Toga-mura.)

This farmhouse theatre we have constructed with Mr. Isozaki's help has become quite well known in many countries around the world, a fact that in turn helped make the establishment of the Toga International Festival a reality.

I have become extremely fond of the theatre, and not just because of the experiences I had in France. There is another reason as well. I am firmly convinced that with the Meiji Restoration in 1868, there came a definite break in the natural historical development of the Japanese theatre. The same kind of break occurred in music and the other arts. The Meiji government put all its political efforts into attempting to catch up with, then surpass, the countries of Europe, which represented for them the standards of high civilization. In music, for example, one need only look at the differences between the kind of music composed before 1868 and the Western-style music studied by modern generations in school. The break was enormous and can be observed in virtually every field.

In the theatre there is an enormous gap between the *nō* and *kabuki* forms on one hand, and the modern Japanese drama on the other. Indeed, *nō* and *kabuki* came to be seen as merely one branch of the theatrical arts, as a classical performing tradition. The modern theatre came to consist of performances of European plays, and what is more, they were usually directed and staged along European lines. Such Western ideas have been applied to the construction of the actual theatre buildings as well. The modern theatre in Japan has thus come to be performed in a kind of "adopted space."

On the other hand, *nō* has scarcely ever been played in such halls. From its beginning as an offering to the gods, *nō* has come to be performed in a special partitioned space, the traditional *nō* stage. The rupture between the traditional and the modern involves more than the contents of the plays being performed; it encompasses the choice of theatrical space to be employed as well. Again and again my thoughts return to reuniting those forms of Japanese theatre which have so recently come to be divided. That is my goal in my work.

Of course, *kabuki* and *nō* are not usable as they are in the modern theatre. There remain splendid concepts and emotions at the very heart of those forms, however, that can be developed in a modern context; and there is great expressiveness in the movements and gestures of those actors who have been tempered through rigorous training. At the same time, under the European influence, a new form of genuine theatrical expressiveness has developed out of the thoughts, fears, and worries of a community that has weathered the fierce changes of our times.

Could not the old and new ways of thinking and feeling be employed in some unified form of theatrical expression? My own activities have been predicated on the belief that there must be a means to truly fuse them, rather than merely grafting on a new branch. The modern theatre has cut itself off from any influence of the *nō* or *kabuki* because those forms are seen as merely old. For a theatre of the future, however, might not some elements be chosen from among all that has been discarded? I certainly believe so. Toward that end, at a time when different troupes rarely perform together, I have worked with such *nō* and *kabuki* performers as Matsumoto Koshiro, Nakamura Senjaku, Kanze Hisao, and Kanze Hideo. They have directed on my stage, and my troupe has worked with them. I hope thereby not only to somehow modernize the traditions of *nō* and *kabuki,* but to study the essential beauties of these forms so as to reintroduce some of their concepts into the contemporary theatre. My ultimate goal is to restore vitality to the theatre in a process similar to that of remodeling an old piece of architecture to order to bring it back to a new and useful life.

Up until recently, I often presented my productions in buildings constructed for European-style performances, such as the Iwanami Hall and the Imperial Theatre in Tokyo. But I began to want to stage my performances in a kind of space familiar and comfortable to the Japanese through the centuries, in order to give new life to those traditional spaces. The idea was in harmony with my own vision of the theatre, and would suit the kinds of plays I was staging. Ultimately, I chose the old farmhouse.

Our mountain home may not be an ideal spot by conventional theatrical or architectural standards, or even in terms of fire prevention; still, it is a space that can give new life to the work we perform there. Pitched roofs or not, we use an old building for our performances, making it possible to incorporate both traditional and contemporary elements into the presentation: the building itself has been reborn. Then, too, I think that the plays performed there might draw a hidden strength from the power of this traditional architecture. That was our first reason for coming to Toga-mura. I say "reborn" because the idea of "re-using" a building implies motives of profit or self interest. I prefer to speak about promoting the "rebirth" of a tradition.

A Performing Space for Theatre

The second reason for establishing a theatre at Toga-mura had to do with the character of the performing space.

In contrast to music, fiction, painting, and other artistic activities, the modern theatre has always been a group endeavor. Most artworks are produced by a single individual. A painter faces the canvas alone, and novelists and composers create in private. Readers and concertgoers do not experience those arts at the same time they are being created. Artists have always done their real work alone, never more so than today.

People seem to look upon artists as somehow special—strange and difficult. And if the term "avant-garde" becomes attached to them as well, the suspicions mount. The artist's lifestyle may seem self-centered, solitary, even antisocial. He may be thought to create his works in an autocratic, altogether personal fashion, unrelated to the society around him.

The theatre, however, cannot be conceived of in such a fashion. In the first place, stage creation necessitates a group effort; and when the work is presented, the spectators become a part of that process, too. As far as I am concerned, no matter how much effort goes into rehearsal, no performance exists without the audience. For me, the theatre is a collective form of artistic expression. In its essence, it involves the establishment of a community of place and time, encompassing both performers and spectators, so that a dialogue may pass between them.

I have a novelist friend who insists that he never knows who may read what he writes. Perhaps only another writer will read him, or a critic, a fact that fills him with a real sense of malaise. And if people do read him, he wonders what impression they will have of his work. He cannot go and ask; his only clue might be an occasional letter. This state-of-being fills him with a terrible sense of loneliness.

A composer, of course, can expect that there will be live performances of his music. In fact, although the system sometimes goes unnoticed, there are methods and mechanisms whereby composers and writers are publicized and the sale of their work is promoted. Professional marketing and promoting organizations make a link between readers, music lovers, and others who wish to experience creative work of this kind; these organizations seek to ascertain in general who these listeners and readers might be, so that the creations of the artists can be made known to them. The artists themselves, of course, have no means to identify their devotees directly.

In contrast, the theatre alone involves an intimate collaboration with its audience during the time of actual creation. Sometimes there are more spectators, sometimes fewer; but in every case the actors, looking out into the auditorium, want to know how many have come and what sort of atmosphere they will create.

It is often said these days that the theatre is in a poor state of health. On the contrary, I find it a flourishing artistic activity, precisely because when a play is performed, a public is there to partake of the experience. In the theatre, a relationship is built up, based on such mutual physical observation, that can lead to a true expressiveness. Only the theatre exhibits these characteristics.

In an age when a mechanized culture is developing rapidly and methods of mechanical reproduction have become increasingly efficient, only the theatre can offer an experience that is never twice the same. We need the theatre because the theatre needs us, a group of live individuals. The experience must be created by a group, functioning just as the theatre has always functioned.

A film can, of course, be copied; even if the writer or the actors are not present, even if it is not known who the spectators will be, a film can be shown all over the entire country simultaneously. For such reasons, film and theatre differ altogether. People often do not distinguish between stage and film performers, simply calling both categories "actors," but I believe there to be a great difference between them.

The modern arts can make use of mechanical means. Those who create the art, though, do so out of their own subjectivity. During the mechanical preparation of such art, audiences need not be present; audience and artists follow their separate trajectories until, on some occasion or other, the two manage to meet. The art that goes furthest in this direction, of course, is the film. Such is perhaps the greatest difference between film and theatre. The process of creating theatre, then, is quite different from that of film, the novel, and music. One definition of the theatre might be that it exists in an "open space." By open space, I do not mean "large," but a space that is only defined by the performance.

In principle an open space does not create itself. Rather, a group of people collects in one spot—they may be eating and drinking together, discussing one thing or another, as though they had all come together as part of a larger conversation. Yet this larger conversation is not altogether unified. Around it various individuals, each in his or her own way, participate in a communal stretch of time with the others. This is the image of "open space" I like to imagine. In my conception, an open space is a place where the individual can take in this random conversation, so that rather than merely examining himself, he can be present in the midst of a group and observe others, noting human differences and similarities. In the kind of open space I have in mind, this dialogue can be encompassed; indeed, the theatre is an ideal place for the dialogue to take place. All who participate can observe what happens on stage, and the spectators can also react among themselves. Such has been the nature of the theatre since the time of the ancient Greeks.

Originally, the Greek theatre was presented out of doors. Theatres like the one at Epidaurus were constructed on the tops of hills. When summer came, people collected in twos and threes to talk and eat in the fields, then watch a play in the open, circular performing space. When the play was finished, they would talk together, drink together, and discuss what they had seen. The spectators asked questions and carried on discussions with the actors.

These ancient traditions are still in evidence today in some places. In Japan, however, for economic efficiency and other reasons, halls for the performance of plays are now built mainly in larger communities. The audience arrives just in time for the curtain to go up. When the presentation is finished, the audience leaves quickly so as not to miss the train home. This has, I believe, severely limited the possibilities of drama in our generation.

If we examine the changes in the theatre since its ancient beginnings, we find that the fundamental concept of a communal art, of drama created in an open space, has become virtually extinct; now, the theatre has become a kind of rite performed in a secret room. That sense of public space has been lost, rendering the art of watching a play quite close to the experience of watching a film or reading a novel. I strongly believe that we must return to open spaces.

Kabuki, like the Greek theatre, was conceived to be performed in open spaces. In that period, when a sensational incident arose, someone committing suicide, for example, the news would appear in print in some form or other. A play on the subject would quickly be mounted on the stage. When an event of the day was dramatized in this fashion, various stories connected to the event would naturally begin to circulate. The spectators would talk among themselves or with the actors; the time spent seeing the play would be fully used, and the plays were not appreciated, as they are today, merely for their artistic content. Audiences went off to the theatre to see what they could find there; they watched, ate, and observed what was happening to their favorite characters. Sometimes they talked politics. The atmosphere was surely very relaxed. Then, people went to the theatre with a variety of expectations, not just for a superb artistic experience. What to buy on the way? What clothes to wear? What to eat there? Would there be a chance to meet some unexpected friend? Each member of the audience planned to use the time before and after the performance for his or her own purposes, and the pleasure of the theatre included all of these things as well.

If a discussion with an audience were to be planned after a play in Tokyo today, however, the promoters would have to hire the hall for the extra time required; this would involve a large sum of money and so pose economic difficulties. As for the spectators, if they missed their trains they would be forced to go home by taxi, and since most of them live in the ever-expanding

.suburbs, the price would be prohibitive. In practical terms, then, for reasons of economic efficiency, theatre can be performed only on a small scale and in as brief a time as possible, for an audience that watches, then departs very quickly. The luxury of leisure must be purchased. Both money and time are hindrances to the conduct of ordinary daily life.

I have been in the business of presenting plays for some years but even so, in Tokyo, there is no possibility of my arranging for an exchange of views with an audience or with the critics, except under very special circumstances. And because the halls are only opened from fifteen to thirty minutes before the start of a performance, there is nothing for the spectators to do but roam around near the theatre or do some shopping on their own. They must spend their time in isolation.

I hope to bring a sense of public space back into the Japanese theatre. Such things as eating, greeting friends, talking, even watching the actors eat are in fact everyday experiences. If audiences can experience these things when going to see a play, they will not only feel that it has some connection to their own lives, but they will sense at the same time that they are stepping into a somewhat different atmosphere. This new sensation, something perhaps approaching the spirit of a holiday, will enter into their consciousness and buoy them up; they will begin to examine themselves from new and unusual angles. This is the kernel of the excitement involved in watching a play. Through the creation of this atmosphere, people will begin to contemplate their own actions. The confluence of those diverse activities taking place in one spot constitutes the kind of public space I dream of.

Such a public space cannot be created in Tokyo. There is no place there or in any city like it where a person, whether he sees a given performance or not, can feel at ease, free from *ennui*. Because the environment is so important, a place must be chosen in the middle of nature, where man can feel free. I believe that such conditions for a theatre can be fully met at Toga-mura. When I first came to that conclusion I called my supporters together from all over the country in order to explain my ideas to them. About six hundred people from virtually all over the country wished me well, and raised the money to support a series of performances over a five-year period. So it was that I began my work at Toga-mura six or seven years ago.

Of course, people visited Toga-mura from all over Japan. And when the performances were finished they often stayed on in the dormitories. The discussions would start. Visitors got up early in the morning, walked around the theatre, even peeked inside. And because their movements were not restricted until just before the beginning of a performance, they could talk with the actors and backstage personnel. The members of the audience started to introduce themselves to one another. They would begin to make acquaintances, to find themselves eating together.

In this kind of theatrical environment, the audience actually helps to shape theatrical time. In a sense, the performers are no longer the only ones with a conscious plan to organize the fixed time that is available.

I would like to add one more thought concerning the concept of a public space. The fact that the theatre possesses communal characteristics means that, to a considerable degree, a quality that I might term "the accidental" comes into play.

In modern life, and so in the dramatic art that forms a part of modern culture, there is a basic, unarticulated assumption that the unexpected must be suppressed. It should come as no surprise that modern civilization has found ways to eliminate the accidental: After all, if high-speed trains or airplanes attempted to incorporate the unexpected, there would be many large-scale accidents. Contemporary culture is committed to the inevitable; everything must be measured; each calculation must be pushed to its conclusion. This pursuit inevitably involves the suppression of the natural and the accidental. We no longer live with nature; we fight with nature and search for the means to subjugate it. Cultural progress has actually become that process of subjugation, and the so-called civilized nations have developed on the basis of those principles.

Let me take the simplest of examples. In an "advanced" country, the regulation of indoor air temperature and humidity is taken for granted. Even the air we breathe has been civilized, "homogenized." Everything is always the same—temperature, humidity, the whole environment is controlled and evened out. If something unexpected happens to this homogenized air, all sorts of problems arise. To prevent this, considerable human ingenuity has gone into finding a means to impose control. Cultural progress, then, is the triumph of the inevitable over the spontaneous.

In the case of the arts, however, and particularly the theatre, the artists involve their whole selves, their living bodies, in a collective performance. The premise is that to foster expressive movement, not every aspect of the performance *can* be planned. In this regard, the performance of a play is quite unlike the playing of a phonograph recording or the viewing of a film. Performance times are never quite the same. A one-hour piece will never end in precisely sixty minutes. It may vary by fifteen seconds, even by five minutes. On the other hand, if you buy a novel, you don't expect the number of pages to swell or the number of printed lines to dwindle.

In the theatre, part of this assumption of the presence of chance involves the audience, which differs every day in appearance, in physiology, in number. This renders the relationship of the spectators to the stage different at every performance. Of course, theatre people do think through their performances as completely as possible, but they realize at the same time that their collective consciousness is built on a foundation that allows for the spontaneous and the accidental. In a sense, the very plans they make become a means of enjoying the fundamental spontaneity of their art.

The Coexistence of Theatre and Nature

The concept of managing the spontaneous in order to control human responses cannot be a part of the process of theatre. People assembled in a theatrical space cannot be controlled. The very performing space makes it impossible.

Looking at this from another angle, theatrical form must in some fashion recognize the spontaneous, and that recognition in itself constitutes an element of protest against the conditions of our contemporary society. The theatre encourages human spontaneity to the maximum and makes no attempt to control feelings or physiology. Medical science, however hard it tries, can never predict everything. The theatre assumes the presence of spontaneous human beings within its creative process. The artform becomes a means for its audience to discover such spontaneity in one form or another and, by making use of it, to create in turn an even more enriched art. Scientists can only attempt to banish that spontaneity.

When something spontaneous or unexpected happens in the course of human affairs, how can it be enjoyed, put to use in the midst of our lives? How can we be made to contemplate the human condition? The power of the artist can do this for us. Yet in our time, the theatre has been relegated to an atmosphere in which the unexpected is less and less possible, and this atmosphere in turn has made our theatre dull. I want, therefore, to return the theatre to its former, spontaneous state.

If the sound of wind or rain penetrates the walls of a modern theatre, we experience the sensation as disagreeable. Many of us, myself included, actually find ourselves becoming angry. "The building isn't constructed properly! The play's spoiled!" Yet at Toga-mura, in a farmhouse, we often hear the sound of rain during a performance, and the wind actually comes in through the cracks. Out in nature as we are, the voices of the frogs can be heard as well. How surprising that no one is annoyed, no one objects.

As the place of performance changes, so do the feelings concerning it. In the atmosphere of Toga-mura, there is no way to quiet the frogs. Or perhaps we have merely adjusted ourselves to the situation—there is virtue in that, too. The theatre can seek to absorb itself into its surroundings in order to develop an appropriate symmetry.

When ways of thinking shift, everything else can change. When the rains fall, we find ourselves performing in one fashion; if the wind blows, we seem to increase the energy we expend in performance all the more. For the spectator and performer alike, nature is no longer to be fought against but is a partner to be lived with and enjoyed. In that relationship, a new and remarkable expressivity becomes possible.

In traditional Japanese garden design, the guiding principle has always been that the elements planned by man must exist in harmony with nature. Modern architecture has changed our perceptions of this completely, so that it is now only in an outdoor theatre or a farmhouse playing space that we can enjoy the sound of the wind or the rain. We who speak of the existence of spontaneity must live in nature not with an attitude of wonder but with a sense of natural pleasure and enjoyment.

The other day, an English troupe performed here and used a whole ski run for its theatrical playing space, which of course made the company completely dependent on the weather. As it turned out, it began to rain in the middle of the performance. Even so, not one member of the audience left. Everyone stayed until the very end. There were children performing and they too continued right on, soaked though they were. After the play ended, some audience members responded by saying, "We had no idea that rain falling during a performance could be so *theatrical.*" Actually, the play and the rain had nothing to do with each other. Under other circumstances, most people would have been annoyed at rain falling during a performance; on this occasion, however, the audience learned something new about the sense of falling rain. They experienced the rain afresh, making a connection they had never made before. Others said, "The sound of the voices in the rain was so emotionally exciting!" They were not troubled by a fixed response to rain falling or not falling, wind blowing or not blowing during a performance. Rather, they communicated with nature in a very real way, and one that had not been determined beforehand. The essence of a real theatrical experience came to the fore: What can a spectator discover at one particular place, at one particular time? How can he come to experience in a new way the environment in which he finds himself? To feel something in a new way, to respond freshly, is not a question of experiencing the unusual in the common sense of the word. Rather, it is to discover something profoundly new in the midst of everyday life. To create a space in which the human sensibility is susceptible to being opened up is a task only the theatre at its best can undertake.

Of course, all of us must live our lives with the help of a certain amount of conscious planning and organization. But every aspect of life cannot be planned. We must always realize the extreme value of the spontaneous and the unexpected. When we die, we return to the earth. So we have no reason to struggle with nature. We must wrap ourselves in nature, live together harmoniously with it. I chose Toga-mura because when our troupe performs there, in the midst of nature, we experience these sensations, as it were, inside our very skins.

As modern culture develops in all its aspects around the world, it seems that the heart is losing any place that it can truly call a home. Yet I firmly believe that such a home is necessary if any human group is to accomplish its purposes. My troupe has always encompassed between thirty and forty people. For the past ten years we have used Tokyo as a base from which to perform all over Japan, and sometimes abroad; often we have made use of modern stages and halls for our presentations. Up until now we have never in our long experience together been able to find any base that might be considered our real home. As theatre people we do not, of course, seek a home in the usual sense of the word: We do not search for mothers or a place to be brought up. We seek a place where as a group we can really perform in the way we wish, a place that we can always carry in our hearts even when we go elsewhere; we need a place that can serve as a source of inspiration and stimulation. Members of the troupe come from all over the country, yet in our theatre work, just as in any similar activity, we need a sense of a communal home. This is just as important to the group as an individual home is to each one of us personally. And it is why I chose Toga-mura, in the hope that it might fulfill this function. This is my third reason for choosing to come here: I wanted to create an environment in which to carry on our work.

Sacred Time, Worldly Time

My next point is a bit more complicated to explain. It seems that all around the world religion is judged to be less important than it has ever been before. In Europe and America the power of Christianity is gradually lessening, and a number of new religions have sprung up to replace it. Many of them are linked to money-raising schemes of one sort or another, and there are even groups like the People's Temple whose members have voluntarily killed themselves. It would seem that as American civilization grows more advanced, the human heart reacts by growing desolate, so that human beings feel the need to seek out some sort of spiritual prop. Based on my own experiences abroad, I've begun to worry that Tokyo, indeed all Japan, will follow the same path. Today, anything resembling an ideal that encourages belief in a religious or spiritual dimension is fast disappearing.

There is another aspect to this issue. According to Mircea Eliade, the great Romanian scholar of Indian and other religions, the further away mankind attempts to push religion, the more we contrive to perform acts that reveal an unarticulated, hidden religious element. The religious aspects of life remain hidden deep in the human heart, and on occasion those concealed currents suddenly reveal themselves. This occurs when, for example, something unpleasant happens in the midst of the most ordinary circumstances: when a person first meets someone with whom he falls in love; when he looks out at the seashore from a train window; or perhaps when he seeks to visit the old house where he played as a child. Even if we are not fully cognizant of such moments, they occur in everyone's life. Indeed, mankind actually seeks the cracks or fissures in the long expanse of time that constitutes his daily life. In Eliade's view, mankind could not live without the quest for such openings.

Eliade refers to these long stretches of daily life as *worldly time*. In this mode, human connections are evaluated in terms of their utilitarian aspects, of the potential for economic exchange; life is led as a form of habit. *Sacred time,* on the other hand, affords a break in worldly time. The term does not refer merely to the kind of "religious time" spent in visiting temples and churches. Man cannot live without ruptures or openings through worldly time and into sacred time, and if any given life is observed closely, it soon becomes apparent that we all find such moments, whether or not we are conscious of them.

All men and women carry on such subterranean religious behavior, and it is manifested and reflected in peculiar ways, through unusual interests. In extreme form, these attitudes are revealed in the way that people cling to things, devote themselves to things. According to Eliade, a person, if asked the reasons for his actions, will reply that he cannot endure the even movement of his everyday life and so seeks a rupture or break in the flow.

It would seem that those of us in the theatre live altogether in the realm of worldly time. In the course of a lengthy evolution, the art of the *nō* actor has become formalized and performers receive a fixed status. *Kabuki* actors now belong to prestigious arts committees and are granted national prestige. Yet, to speak bluntly, they were and are part of what we call a service industry. Theatrical performers are meant to give their all in order to bring pleasure to others. Theatrical activity is not to be engaged in for the benefit of the performers but should grow from a desire to satisfy others. An actor uses his body as a means to express his own suffering, pain, and joy; he strives to create a community with those who participate in his performance. His joy is a joy to be shared; his sadness exists to make his audience all the sadder; if he sees another smiling, he feels that happiness himself. Nothing could be more satisfying for an actor than to bring joy to others. Such are the impulses of theatre performers, and a life away from others cannot be imagined.

No actor can give a performance alone and for himself. (The only possible exception might be some temple dancer, a priestess to a deity.) But by what means can the actor's joy or his sadness be conveyed to others? How to explain his pain of living? How to bring happiness to another? How, in a short space of time, to carry out such a diversion? In the actor's head, the others are always present. Leading one's life while always thinking of others means living with everything continually unresolved, unsettled. So, as far as the purity of one's spiritual state is concerned, those in the theatre—who always have those others in their heads—must understand that they lead their lives in worldly time and with very worldly feelings.

In this particular sense, any endeavor that can be classed as a service industry is very much involved in worldly time; every nō actor from Zeami onwards has felt a kind of self-loathing at the need to find his significance through the consciousness of others. Nō actors were once called beggars in the riverbeds; now they are members of arts committees and have become National Treasures, a treatment far different from any they had known before. Yet, however famous a performer becomes, it is difficult for him to face another person, for he retains a sense that his profession is somehow inferior. On the other hand, the fact that he can bring pleasure to so many prompts him to feel a kind of self-conceit as well, so that pride and inferiority become mixed together. Indeed, any performer who cannot live with these two competing feelings is probably not worthy of the name actor.

[89]

An actor must always bring himself face to face with others; emotionally, he is never in a state of relaxation. In order to reach a spiritual state where he can live in peace with himself, many an actor has decided in the end that he cannot go on being called the such-and-such-generation Danjurō, like some sort of white monkey—and so has thrown over his career altogether.

Our troupe performs all around Japan and even appears occasionally on television. In order to keep the troupe from disintegrating, some kind of home, some source of authority is needed. This space is not for the sake of the spectators but for the sake of our own performers, to enable them to work to their utmost abilities.

Our work in the theatre is not only spiritual; our task requires the use of our bodies as well. Thus there must be available to us a theatrical space that the body can remember. In this regard, I learned a great deal from studying the *nō* stage. At the very instant an actor enters the performing space on a traditional *nō* stage, his body transforms itself.

Nō has its own stage, and the *nō* actors always rehearse in the same space. An actor who enters onto any traditional stage therefore finds himself in familiar territory, amidst the same arrangement of walls and pillars, so that his body always feels in accord with the playing space. The nature of that space is so much a part of his being that even if he could no longer use his eyes, he would never fall off the stage.

Actors in the modern theatre, however, have to cope one day with a small theatre in a private hall and the next with a huge stage in some prefectural cultural center. Sometimes they must perform in a vast television studio having rehearsed in a tiny, restricted space. The actor who must move about in such worldly spaces, in which his body can find no basic authority, will find no support for his movements. As a result his body will not be able to put up any resistance to changes and will simply weaken as it attempts to adapt to every arbitrary change in theatrical space.

On the basis of our performing overseas, I can certainly say that the biggest difficulty we face comes from the great diversity in the size of theatres. Halls sometimes turn out to be half the size we were led to anticipate, and a theatre described as a semi-circular "open stage" may turn out to be a completely round "arena stage."

The actors, responding to these diverse spaces, must adjust their bodies on every occasion, a fatiguing process indeed. They feel somewhat as I do when I am interviewed by newspaper reporters. One after another comes and goes; because I have no idea how much they know or understand of my work when I talk to them, no real communication is possible. On any given day there may be ten or more different reporters, each with a different degree of knowledge, each asking questions based on his own preconceptions. To be interviewed in this fashion can be exhausting.

Similarly, actors must put forth a tremendous effort in order to change themselves to suit those different spaces. Because *nō* actors have a fixed space available to them which they have internalized into their very bodies, they instinctively move on any stage as though it were a *nō* stage. The actor's body and the space reveal a mutual connection. I call a space which is thus connected to the actor's body a *sacred space*.

To put my idea another way, there exists within the bodies of those *nō* actors a fundamental repertoire of gestures that constitutes a whole standard of performance. Therefore, wherever they perform they can easily gauge the relation of their bodies to the playing space available. There already exists within the body of the *nō* actor the kind of space that can force a rent in the flow of worldly time. *Kabuki* has lost this quality because its own similar base has disappeared. *Nō,* of course, is an extremely sophisticated artform. The easiest way to destroy it would be to take away that special stage. Without the discipline necessitated by such a space, the *nō* would quickly become an extremely uninteresting form of theatre.

Nō actors, through their childhood training, gain an intimate sense of this sacred element in their art, and the *nō* stage, which serves as a standard against which to measure these feelings, stands as the marvelous theatrical invention crowning the whole aesthetic. Japan may possess the only theatre in the world in which the design of the stage itself is part of the basic conception, and our own modern theatre troupes would do well to embrace such a concept. My actors must have the kind of spiritual home that can permit them to understand me when I say, "This stage is your body's real home. Whatever the shape or structure of a stage you may be called to perform on, this home remains your standard, your basis for judgment."

Without this sense, and with no real standards, actors move from hall to theatre, looking vaguely at the spaces before adjusting their performances in too casual a manner. These actors run the risk of approaching straw and wood in the same fashion that they approach concrete, without considering the possibility of differing responses. All their energies will thus be scattered in worldly time, and the audience will have only the most flimsy and superficial experience of such a performance. The actors' own bodies will appear weak and unsteady. Their sense of their existence will quickly disappear.

Animals exhibit the same tendencies. The Austrian zoologist and writer Konrad Lorenz, in describing the energizing of the body, remarks that when he watches animals quarreling, it is possible to determine from their demeanor whose territory is at stake. According to Lorenz, when a dog's territorial boundaries are broached, there is a fight and the one that "loses" runs away; yet if the winning dog advances too far out of his own territory, he too will weaken and have to retreat. A dog becomes stronger and stronger as he moves to the center of his own territory, but weaker and weaker as he moves away into other areas. Whether he "wins" or "loses" depends on the territory involved. The outcome does not simply depend on the relative strength of the dogs; that strength must be related in turn to a sense of security, which grows stronger as the dog approaches the center of his own home territory.

Human beings function in much the same way. Actors need the safety of a base; it is just as though they were returning to the tranquility of their own houses.

Modern theatres in Japan are usually owned by people who have no connection to the theatre. In Tokyo, for example, the Nissei Theatre is owned by an insurance company, and the well-known Kinokuniya Hall is run by a large bookstore. These are multi-purpose stages, not designed solely for theatrical performances. In Japan, only the *nō* stage was conceived and planned by the actors themselves. All the rest were planned by the entertainment industry, with profit-making the motive. These theatres are designed to accommodate as many spectators as possible, and to provide for a variety of non-theatrical activities. As far as I am concerned, such theatres cannot provide a real home base, for they do not embody the kind of sacred space the actors require.

During my travels I decided that I must somehow find a proper spot in which to create the kind of space my actors long for, however poor and simple it might have to be. It was in such a frame of mind that we came to occupy our modest farmhouse theatre. There are doubtless some who will maintain that these buildings do not really constitute a theatre. Yet I really do believe that at Toga-mura we have created, as actors, a special theatre with our own needs in mind.

The International Festival at Toga-mura

The issues I have raised have all been explored now. At this point, I would like to answer the question put to me by so many reporters and journalists: Why do we hold an international theatre festival here, rather than somewhere such as Tokyo?

First of all, and without boasting, I really do believe that Toga-mura is probably the only place where such a festival could be held in Japan today. There is no other stage constructed to offer so many possibilities. Most of Japan's stages are copies of Western models, designed for multiple use. Such theatres, planned in terms of contemporary culture, do not really permit the close, physical, personal contact needed. Thus the basic theatrical experience is inevitably weakened. A similar problem exists in Europe: The kinds of theatres available in the larger cities there now seem to offer limited theatrical possibilities also. In France, nationally sponsored theatre companies are moving to the provinces, and there is a clear trend away from holding important festivals in large cities. In the U.S., those truly conscientious avant-garde performers who feel most keenly the dangers of today's world, who wish to reflect that concern in their theatre, are beginning to abandon their commitment to New York. In Japan, we look on Toga-mura as a kind of last resort.

Next comes the matter of economics.

In Tokyo, the cost of hiring a hall for theatrical performances is very high indeed. Economic efficiency and money-making must come before any other considerations. A month of performances at the Imperial Theatre in Tokyo, for example, costs between thirty and forty million yen (close to $140,000). Much, much more would be involved in running a two-month international festival. There has been talk of sponsoring such a festival in Tokyo, and one regional area has made an attempt as well. Yet as the theatre depends for its success on close and intimate communication with a small number of spectators, there is no way to succeed in a large urban area if economic efficiency remains the central consideration. In order to ensure a profit, ticket prices must be inordinately high. For reasons such as these, no plan for a festival in a large urban area in Japan has ever succeeded.

It was because of such situations that we decided to hold our festival at Toga-mura.

Fortunately, it turned out that, since I have often worked

abroad—participating in theatre festivals outside of Japan, and even teaching for a considerable time at an American university—I have come to know a number of theatre people around the world. I asked many of them how they would like to bring their troupes to my home, as it were. They answered yes, they would love to do it. They asked for no fees; they just wanted to give it a try. One after another, they came. Their response was much more positive than I had expected.

One English company performed for only three days at Toga-mura and then returned home. Yet the British government was willing to invest a large sum in this brief visit. When I asked if it would be necessary for them to perform in Tokyo as well, they told me, "Not at all. This kind of performance wouldn't make any sense except in a place like Toga-mura. Don't worry, we'll just turn around and go back." Being Japanese, I was really startled by their answer. Most Japanese theatre people would not understand such logic at all. Our general attitude would be to give performances to as wide a variety of spectators as possible, and in a city like Tokyo, where the interest in theatre is strong. The English, however, viewed the issue this way: "Don't worry. We want to visit Toga. We only want to perform for the kind of audience that can appreciate what we are trying to do. There may be a greater knowledge of the arts in Tokyo, but that's really not the point. The question these days is not of quantity but of quality; the size of the audience doesn't worry us at all. As far as the artists are concerned, even if a lot of money is spent just so that one person may be deeply moved by our performance, then cultural exchange is worthwhile. We don't require a broad introduction of our troupe. We are hoping to achieve a mutuality of human feeling; when people come together for these reasons, we don't need any performance fees."

Some companies, like a Polish troupe that visited recently, must take a different attitude. "We must do anything we can to perform in Tokyo. Because of the political situation at home, we really need the money to take back with us." They, of course, were able to do so. Most of the visiting troupes get into a real give-and-take with us. "My home is in Toga-mura. Won't you come and visit?"

"Why not? Let's give it a try."

Many people ask me why, when visitors come from abroad, I don't take them to expensive restaurants in Tokyo. Why not entertain them at the Okura Hotel, the Imperial Hotel? Why do I feed them simple country food? When I invite friends from abroad to Japan, I tell them in advance that our resources are limited, and I do not feel that they should be given unrealistic treatment. Besides, even those fancy hotels are limited—there are lots of authentic Japanese dishes they can't provide!

Perhaps at my home I cannot offer the sumptuous things that a hotel might. But I try to respond to the real needs of my visitors as best I can. And the theatre companies I invite don't hesitate to ask for what they need. We have taken down walls, put up extra pillars. And we can do this at Toga-mura because it *is* our home.

In order to welcome our friends, we think it important to undertake such projects cheerfully; we do not believe that we should make a choice as to how to treat them while looking over a menu at some fancy hotel. Meeting the needs of our fellow artists is the warmest kind of welcome we can give them. An empty show of friendship is of no use at all. European artists and men of culture are bored by bombastic celebrations. According to them, when they arrive in Japan they are always given parties, yet the guests are financiers and politicians who have nothing to say to artists. All they can do is to exchange business cards and go home. What a surprising country Japan is, they say. Under such circumstances, it has always seemed to me, real cultural exchange is virtually impossible. For that reason, I have always tried to find a means by which a real correspondence between the two countries involved can be made possible, however limited the means at our disposal. Toga-mura seemed absolutely the best place to prepare a truly proper welcome and so I decided to open my international festival there. Fortunately, my invitations were accepted and the festival came into being without difficulty. If a festival such as ours had been staged in a resort area such as Karuizawa, Nagano, or Shizuoka, it would have become merely a kind of mini-Tokyo attraction. I really believe that Toga-mura itself makes our festival unique. At this point, then, the question "Why Toga-mura?" has been answered.

I would like to add that we have been able to establish our international theatre festival through the financial assistance of Toyama Prefecture. I myself now make my official residence in Toyama and plan to continue my cultural activities there indefinitely.

5

Empty Village

Next year [1983] will mark a decade since I first began my activities at Toga-mura.

I did not go there because I had to leave Tokyo. Indeed, I did not leave Tokyo thinking that I would carry on no more activities there; the thought never crossed my mind.

At first, journalists and theatre people in Tokyo teased me a great deal. Was I going to become a Buddhist recluse, they asked, or was I escaping off into the wilderness to become a native? Local papers asked how long I could last out there; wasn't this, perhaps, just a momentary fling? And wouldn't all our imported urban culture throw this mountain village into disorder and confusion? Some of the villagers, in fact, when they first saw certain members of our troupe in beards and overalls, may well have thought we were the Japanese Red Army coming to carry out our maneuvers in a borrowed farmhouse.

There was nothing we could do to counteract those feelings. After all, there was no one living in the immediate vicinity. We could practice until late at night without anyone taking notice; only the foxes and badgers might complain.

I have explained our attitudes on a number of occasions and so do not need to provide any more details here; suffice it to say that I had always disliked the fact that our activities were limited to Tokyo. In that sense, any suitable place outside of the capital would have done as well as Toga. My feelings had been the same when we first set up the Waseda Little Theatre in Shinjuku. We had not established ourselves there because we had found a performing space that somehow matched our ideal expectations. It had really happened more or less by accident.

Although one person may set out to make a personal choice, it is never freely done. He is forced to make decisions based on a set of specific, limited circumstances. This was true even when I undertook to establish the Waseda Little Theatre. At that time in my career when, frankly speaking, I was least likely to compromise my desires, I still found myself under the most severe restrictions. If, in my various activities as a director, my public has not always sensed these limitations, it may be because I persist in making the kind of choices that lead to my being surprised at what I discover. It is that sense of surprise which I find myself speaking about and occasionally writing about.

We in the theatre are faced with so many shifting conditions. We may have enough money or too little; our theatres may be vast or tiny; we may have large audiences or small ones. Reviewers may praise or dislike our work. Yet, whatever the external conditions, as long as we have the resources to mount our work on the stage, we can work toward our goals with all our might; and if we persist in our chosen actions, we can make certain discoveries because of them. Will we adhere to what we find or not? Will there be value in what we discover? Whatever the answers, any progress that we can make is based, I firmly believe, on our maintaining a sense of surprise at what we learn. In any case, I continue to stick to what I am learning at Toga-mura, to believe in it, and I assume that I will do so for the rest of my career. All this was by no means clear when I first began.

How did I become committed to Toga-mura? For one thing, in much the same way that I had made discoveries about the art of performance during our time in Shinjuku, I came in contact at Toga-mura with a new kind of space; our farmhouse theatre there made possible a special closeness to nature. I continued to follow the implications of what I discovered. It was a great shock indeed for me to learn that what I want is to continue my explorations and discoveries in this space until I die. Of course, part of my conviction lies in the knowledge that in Japan today, there are no opportunities for me to create a theatre that might be more suitable to my troupe, no chance for me to have a space constructed altogether in accordance with my wishes. If we were to limit this discussion to questions of theatrical space, I might feel quite differently if a patron should appear who would build a theatre precisely to my specifications. I'm naturally greedy, of course; with Toga-mura as a base, why not construct theatres to my design in New York, Paris, Aomori, or Kagoshima?

Our troupe does occasionally perform in such commercial spaces in Tokyo as the Imperial Theatre or the Iwanami Hall. In these instances, we are only too grateful when the available space involves as little compromise as possible. Nevertheless, we must struggle against criticism when we perform in such places. If we perform in the Iwanami Hall, we are taken to task as though we were *nō* performers who should be performing out of doors, as was originally the case, who had now become slaves of an academic approach to the theatre; if we perform at the Imperial Theatre, we are accused of having sacrificed art to commerce. Actually, when any theatrical work is staged anywhere in Japan, it becomes clear that actors are full of bad habits. Even if the actual content of a piece is maintained, any alteration in the methods of performance, made to satisfy shifting conditions, inevitably brings with it a certain sloppiness. And when the performance concerned becomes academic as well, or thoroughly commercial, the problems are all the more pronounced. There is no merit for the performers, it would seem, in attempting to avoid these dangers.

In any terms you care to set down for commercial success in the theatre, our activities at Toga-mura fall into the red. We are held together by a kind of volunteer spiritual support that could only characterize a group with religious convictions. There are roughly forty members in the troupe. We work in a place where the villagers themselves are struggling for their own existence and have no leisure time for the theatre; no matter how many months we might perform, we could never manage to be economically self-sufficient on the basis of support by local audiences. Nor can the village itself be self-sufficient. The yearly budget of the village is over $7 million, of which ninety-five percent is supplied by the central government. Like our theatre group, the village itself must attract money from the authorities in Tokyo for its support.

Japan is an advanced industrial country. Anyone in our culture who has found himself manipulated by economic considerations will not be surprised that our theatrical activities at Toga-mura cannot be sustained merely by our excitement over a sense of space.

There is another factor to be considered as well. Toga-mura is surely a classic case of an underpopulated area. I am, of course, neither a government official nor a political scientist, but as I see the problem, the population is leaving the area in large numbers, causing the village to lose its ability to govern itself. Villages all around the country seem to be thinning out in this manner. There is nothing to stop the villagers from leaving; so now a very few people find themselves living on a large area of land. This thinning-out phenemenon is particularly obvious in our present period of advanced economic growth. As a result of the revolution in sources of energy, Japanese society has become industrialized, and prosperity has caused an accumulation of people in large urban centers. As Japan has moved toward a dependence on oil, electricity, and gas, the villagers who once provided firewood, coal, and charcoal have lost their livelihoods.

As the cities have swelled in size, the secondary and tertiary industries have grown as well, so that the villagers who lost their jobs in such primary fields as farming and forestry have begun to flock to the cities in search of work. The development of a transportation network and a mass communications system has helped urbanize the consciousness of the villagers themselves, thus encouraging a still greater exodus to the cities. It is said that the era of rapid economic growth is now at an end, and that we are in a period when these developments are being questioned, but there has been no change as yet in the phenomenon of the thinning out of these mountain villages.

The area occupied by Toga-mura is between 500 and 600 meters above sea level. It runs twenty-three kilometers from east to west and fifty-two kilometers from north to south. About forty percent of this area is suitable for housing, yet at this time there are only 332 households in the area, with a total of about 1,200 inhabitants. The principal sources of employment for these families include the city office, a forest and agricultural cooperative, and an engineering company. Indeed, the city office remains the largest employer, providing jobs for nearly 100 people. Young people, especially young women, move away as they marry, so the population is inevitably growing older. The fierce weather, too, makes the life of this aging population more difficult. In the winter, the packed snow is at least three meters deep and can reach a depth of six meters when snowfalls are heavy. In this heavy snow belt, the snow can slide from the roofs of houses with such force that victims can be killed. As the population grows older, many come to depend on the income of their sons and daughters working in the city, and so they leave the village themselves. Houses abandoned by such families dot the hillsides. As the winters go by, these houses disappear one by one, crushed by the weight of the snow. It is hard to describe the sense of desolation this creates. When I first came to the village, of course, I knew nothing of all this. The first thought that the members of our company, still so young, could express was a desire to tell all their parents to come and build houses here, in the middle of this beautiful natural setting with its splendid old farmhouses.

During my university days, twenty-five years ago, the French philosopher Jean-Paul Sartre had an enormous influence on my generation. In Sartre's view, mankind should gather its strength to battle on with the pride of the defeated, even if the future looks none too bright. He said a number of wise things concerning man's consciousness of the emptiness of the human condition. I was much impressed with his concept that man gains his stature by battling on, always in the face of such knowledge. Sartre's ideas were appreciated by the young of my generation, who, although they harbored their dreams, had already felt themselves subjectively and psychologically wounded. We all wanted to live our individual human lives to the fullest, yet each of us found himself pulled among various forces. Nothing we could choose seemed truly worth dying for. Or we could only find ways to live that were at considerable variance with our own beliefs; and although we felt we had to give in to this, the question remained as to what extent we could take control of our own humanity, to what extent we could comprehend the need to do battle. We believed that, although we might not feel a sense of regret if we could not accomplish what we set out to do, we should struggle so as not to regret never having *tried* to do anything. Sartre said such things in a humanistic context that was somewhat different from our own frame of mind, yet we interpreted his words to suit our purposes, and they meant a great deal to us.

Modern man's self-consciousness has required that he consider his humanity deliberately, but this does not mean that he will necessarily find consistency in his own humanity. Quite the contrary. Man must make his life in terms of the circumstances in which he finds himself. He can go through his daily existence according to a variety of standards.

Our life exists in close relationship to the arbitrary, the unexpected. It is multi-layered. In striving for consistency we may try to banish chance or reduce various aspects of life to a single dimension. Even so, we can find no means to narrow down our own future; it is as if we were horses racing along one straight line.

What we can do is seek to develop a self-consciousness of the character of our own activities. These activities in turn must be dictated by our determination to carry on our own inquiries with sincerity. And our inquiries are formed by our point of view on the situation of our time. To put it more simply, we must struggle on with a clear vision of our situation as we find it; living in the world means joining in with the rest of its disillusioned, chilled humanity. No one merely lives in a private world of his own; he must look beyond his own individuality in order to comprehend the meaning of his existence in a larger universe.

When I observe those villagers who have remained behind at Toga-mura, I see them as men and women who are actually living out this struggle of the defeated. Yet I also know that at some point even they will be forced to leave. Even if their situation improves, what with the rigors of the environment, worries over education and medical care, and the lack or recreational facilities, they will eventually be attracted to urban life as they imagine it. Looking at all the conditions of village life, there is really no way to stem the thinning out of its population. In the primary school, there is roughly one student per grade. Ten students, representing all the grades, huddle together to do their work. No wonder the woman who has come up from the city to marry someone in the village feels such an inevitable sense of desolation when she sees them. The more they learn, the more foolish it seems; and even if one argues that their level of study need not be based on their actual calendar age, there seems no reason for them to develop their powers of reasoning.

The work of the mayor in a village like this is to develop a plan to keep the number of people who leave to a minimum. To accomplish this, he petitions for financial aid from one agency after another, starting with the Toyama Prefect authorities and going on to the Construction Ministry and the Ministry of Agriculture and Forestry. As mayor he must know even as he issues these petitions that they cannot be altogether effective. Yet he cannot simply sit by and wait. As long as one person still wants to live in the village, it is his duty to improve the environment there as much as possible. He cannot stand by, lamenting the situation. He must try what he can. Successive village heads have, in fact, been successful in diminishing the exodus a little, but no one has been able to stop it. From an outsider's point of view, the mayor's duty is like that of Camus' Sisyphus, or, to put it another way, like the efforts of a bicycle rider who must keep everything in perilous balance. The mayor, more than anyone else, must fight the fight of the defeated with all his might. He bears the responsibility for the welfare of the whole village.

The mayor's psychological burden is enormous. Any kind of news or information is transmitted directly to him. Surely much of this should not be repeated to the villagers directly. He must find himself lonely indeed.

The scholar Murakami Yasusuki predicts the relationship that will develop between the broad public and the administration in his book *The Appearance of a New Mass Society*. He indicates that, as Japan thrives economically and the concept of individualism and the self becomes even more widely accepted, the majority of people will inevitably become conscious of their personal needs and begin seeking emotional fulfillment and an individual style of life. A desire to sustain self-centered values will arise; as a result, there will be less value placed on such matters as fidelity, hard work, and other larger social concerns. Yet as long as society continues to rely on rationalism and industrialization, the value of rational efficiency cannot lightly be put aside. Thus, the burden on the officials who govern the bulk of the Japanese population will be very great, and they will find themselves psychologically isolated. This is because, in a society such as the one developing in Japan today, the social initiative of the large mass of the population will increase, while the functions of the administrative elite will seem more difficult to justify and so will weaken.

This thesis seems accurate concerning the nations of the so-called advanced world, when comparing their situation to the

Soviet Union and the socialist bloc countries, where the central state remains powerful.

The mayor often jokes that his village is a "consumer's association," but I am sure that this man, who spends half his time every month on the train taking petitions to Tokyo, must feel a terrible emptiness in his heart. After all, how did he come to assume the terrific burden of looking after this tiny bit of countryside, this microcosm of the whole of Japanese society rent apart by the forces of rapid social change?

When I first came to the village, I began to feel in myself this sense of the isolation of the politicians, and the contradictions inherent in the structure of Japanese society. For that reason, I did everything I could to cooperate with the mayor and his policies so as to help reduce the depopulation of the area. Of course, I never intervened directly in any of the political activities in the village, which would have been beyond my powers. Still, I tried to do what I could to help stem the flow of the population and even perhaps to bring about an influx. In such efforts, the presence of our theatre group was essential. It was quite clear to me that if the population declined any further we could no longer perform in Toga-mura, no matter how ideal the surroundings might be for our activities. If the population continued to decline, the very operations of the village would come to a halt. After all, if financial aid or local subsidy taxes were to decrease, transportation facilities would suffer and the ability to remove snow from the roads would be in jeopardy as well, housing would no longer be available, and our theatrical activities would be directly affected.

Let me provide a very specific example. There are no men who cut trees or handle logs in the village. There are only two or three carpenters, in fact. As the mountains are full of trees and anyone may cut them, you might think that the price of wood would be quite reasonable; this is not the case. The expenses of erecting a new structure mount very high indeed, unless imported lumber from the United States or Southeast Asia is used. If the trees near the village are cut, there is no sawmill nearby to use. The logs must be carted off to another town. The costs of workmen and transportation mount, and the price per board-foot of lumber soars. Of course, if there were sufficient demand for wood, a sawmill could be built at Toga-mura, and there would then be loggers and transportation people as well.

As the population leaves, when houses are destroyed, no new ones are built. There is no market for lumber. When we need wood for our theatre we have to drive forty kilometers to buy it in another town. We have the same problem with carpenters. Such difficulties crop up in every aspect of daily life in such a place, so that as the population shrinks, ordinary activities become more and more difficult to carry out. Life in all its aspects becomes very hard to cope with.

Our theatre company cannot set up a plan to run itself as a separate country; if the village of Toga-mura dissolves, our activities there must cease. Such is the close relationship between them. No one in Tokyo can imagine the complexity of relationships in a region such as ours. In fact, most theatre people cannot imagine that Tokyo itself could disappear. They would be surprised at the idea even if it were broached as an abstract proposition. They would find no reality in the word "disappear" itself; such ideas are not part of their daily schedule. I myself really do believe that Tokyo, indeed all of Japan, might truly disappear. There is certainly a strong possibility that the village of Toga-mura might vanish; this is evident in the problems of living there and from the statistics available.

Knowing the situation as I do, why do I restrict my activities to the theatre? If the village is really in danger of disappearing, should I not do my best as a human being to try to help solve the problems of the village, indeed the problems of Japan, with the same energy that I pour into my theatre? Then I would really be accomplishing something of value. Audaciously, I admit that, along with the mayor and those who really love the village, I live as one of those who, while defeated, still battle on.

The idea of living this way, struggling against all obstacles, pushing along at whatever cost, may seem like flirting with the older Japanese ideas of samurai martyrdom, but there are real differences. In many ways, the life of a theatre director actually does resemble the life of someone like the mayor of Toga-mura. We always want to try new things. Even when the human energy at our command seems limited, we put everything we have into what we do.

Without the villagers, the mayor himself does not exist. Without the actors, the director does not exist either. The work of a stage director has no independent life; he is not like other creative artists whose work is aimed directly at the eye or the ear. The theatre director plots out points of connection, intersections; his art is the ability to create balances. He can never remain at any particular point of development, but must move his group toward new discoveries; he maintains for the troupe a relationship with the outside world that is changing yet continuous. In short, the problem the director faces is how to bring about the necessary development of his troupe and, just as important, how to maintain the means to do so. He must continually renew his vision, then work toward it on a trial-and-error basis. He must bring about the communal work with the actors that allows them to change and develop, while growing himself as an individual. The work of the director requires that he build, on the basis of those changes (themselves difficult to stop once set in motion), a larger, future vision. Not only does the object of his concerns change over time; the director himself alters as well. He chooses the actors, the work to be performed, and the place of performance. Even though I am an artistic director, I am responsible in addition for the economic welfare of my troupe. I cannot simply decide what to do based on some personal emotional enthusiasm. I must observe changes in our audiences, even in society itself, and my plans must be based on what I perceive. There is no possibility of my simply amusing myself with my work in some narcissistic fashion.

I live in the world and continue on in the world; I make connections with all things around me. To what extent should I attempt to grapple with those connections? Here is the most difficult problem facing the director, and herein lies his most demanding task. Inevitable connections are formed between the theatre director and other people, between him and the society in which he lives. The director who understands these influences upon him can use that consciousness to make choices that are pleasing to his audiences. Such accomplishments validate the work of a director, providing him a genuine vocation.

Of course, in another sense, the very idea of conscious persistence is perhaps already out of date. One might even argue that such an idea runs counter to the true theatrical act; that a theatre performance springs up and is gone as quickly as it came; that from this impermanence emerges the real theatrical moment, which transcends time. But I myself find that such arguments are themselves out of date. After all, our own lives spring up, then disappear in seventy-odd years. Why should one who has undertaken the unbidden task of working in an ensemble stress the obvious vanity of human wishes? For me, theatrical activity will consist, until the very end of my life, in an attempt to create a deliberate continuity, a mechanism that will bind together the otherwise fitful impulses of actors.

Theatre people in Japan, whatever they may say, do not pursue in any radical way the goal of searching out such a vision, or attempting to use it for purposes of artistic pleasure. Theatre people, like everyone else, are not in themselves methodical; they see the theatre as possessing quite the opposite virtue of spontaneity and so do little more than strike serious and gloomy poses in order to amuse themselves with miniature pleasures. They do not engage themselves with the real emptiness that arises out of the very impossibility of method. They do not really taunt that void, make sport of it. They have never struggled with the energy of the defeated, the true fate of any real theatre director. I only feel in their work a cramped and febrile sense of purpose. The theatrical diversions they create, one after the other, do little more than wound and undercut; they make no attempt to deal with the *nature* of that act of wounding or undercutting, or of the emptiness that lies beyond.

This shallow spirit seems all the more apparent today. As far as I am concerned, it is not surprising to see people so nervously seeking diversions, for, is not the theatre merely "play" after all? By "merely" I do not mean that the theatre is unworthy of serious effort, but that the theatre, like life itself, cannot finally amount to very much, no matter how much energy is expended. I hold that nothing, if not the fiercely sober, existentialist spirit, will ever enable men to work as an ensemble in order to create something of lasting value.

Since coming to Toga-mura, I am most thankful for one thing. Here, I have been able to encounter a certain number of others who take pleasure in what we do because they have become conscious of the limitations of their own humanity; they have come to understand that human activity cannot be regularized, or, to put it another way, that they cannot have things done simply according to their wishes. And yet they are the ones who know how to enjoy life, thriving on that recognition. To parody Sartre's words, I have finally been able to see at close range a few people who truly understand that life is a useless but passionate play, but who are driven by the fact that they too must continue on, to fight the battle of the defeated. All this has become very important to me.

6

Undated Entries from My Diary

The Five Mountains

The people here in Toga-mura have shown me around. I've been to the village, the upper village, and I've even walked as far as the neighboring prefecture of Gifu, all the way over to the village of Shirakawa. I've been driven over a superb road that is referred to as "The Gorge-jumping Farmhouse Line." Through the car windows I saw black tiled roofs against white walls, hillsides dotted with farmers' thatched cottages, and leaves in their temporary fall colors: the very picture of Beautiful Japan at this time of the year. (I suppose the high-speed road is Beautiful Japan as well.)

Toga-mura, in Toyama Prefecture, includes three settlements in addition to the village and upper village; collectively, they are referred to as "The Five Mountains." The first time I heard the expression I assumed that five actual mountains existed, but this is not so. The expression grew out of the fact that originally there were settlements in five valleys, linked together.

This area has become widely known because of folksongs that refer to the unusual farmhouse architecture found here. From the outside everything looks peaceful, but the reality is quite the reverse. Many signs can be seen of the fierce battles the people must wage in order to live in this area, against the violence of nature. Today, the greatest worry is over depopulation. The residents of The Five Mountains are desperately trying to keep their population from vanishing altogether.

The isolation of these mountain villages has been broken by the revolution in energy, the communications network, and the development of the transportation system. People living here feel close to the cities now. They can only conceive of themselves and of the area as a pastime for the city people, who seek out scenic areas for tourism.

Standing here in this spot, with its population fast disappearing, one can feel the stresses and strains of Japanese society as it moves into the phase that follows high-speed industrialization. You don't need to see the facts and figures. You can feel them in your skin.

The Director

Alan Schneider has come up to Toga-mura. He is here for a meeting of artists and scholars brought together to share their views on cultural exchange.

Schneider is famous as a director of Samuel Beckett. In America, he not only puts Beckett on the stage, but has directed a Beckett film as well, featuring Buster Keaton. Schneider was an important teacher for many years at Juilliard, and now teaches at the University of California at San Diego. The acting program at Juilliard includes students from all over the United States. Starting next year, ten students from that group will be chosen to come to Toga-mura for training. Schneider will act as one of the judges to select them, so he has come in person to see the facilities here.

He is an older director, now over sixty, and he dresses in a rather sporty fashion. He gets up early to roam around the stage and the dormitories. And he walks all over Toga-mura. Jean-Louis Barrault and Peter Brook were the same. Foreign directors, it would seem, become increasingly curious as they grow older. Schneider walks a lot. He seems very much taken with the thatched farmhouses and the other buildings here. We have more or less decided to do a new Beckett piece here, with Shiraishi Kayoko, for the 1984 Toga Festival. Schneider will direct. What a fancy spread that will make—Samuel Beckett served up in an old Japanese farmhouse!

Beautiful Violence

It's time for me and the members of the troupe to do our big cleaning at Toga-mura. Every once in a while we discover that straw dust and bits of wood have collected in the spaces above the stage. There are no ceilings in these thatched buildings, which have only open rafters, and when the winds blow through, all this refuse collects. There are also wood-eating insects, who create a fine powder that drops down onto the floor. Above the stage there are thin sheets of anodized aluminum that reflect a dim light; when the wood dust floats nearby, it looks beautiful.

When the cleaning is finished, but before the snow begins to fall, we must put up snow fences all around the windows and entrances. Even the stage itself, in summer so full of the activity of theatre people from so many countries, goes into hibernation. When the buildings are completely surrounded by the snow fences, it is no longer possible for us to enter, and as soon as the snow starts to pile up, it is difficult even to get close. The snow mounts up to a depth of three or four meters, and even as high as six in a heavy fall. The whole theatre seems to be buried in snow. Starting two years ago, until the beginning of last year, so much snow came down from the northern regions of the country that even the roof became difficult to see. On the third of last January, all the employees of the city office came out in force to dig the theatre out of the snow for us. Usually, people talk about throwing snow *down* from a roof; this time, they talked about throwing it *up*. People still use that expression when they refer to that winter. Another farmhouse nearby, used as a meeting hall for the Sokagakkai, had its beams bent by the weight of the snow. Snow is a beautiful form of violence.

This year, the snow came early. The first fall was on October twenty-fifth.

Mosquito Nets

We've decided to perform *The Trojan Women* in its revised version at the Sōgetsu Hall in Tokyo, so the staff and I have begun looking around to see what scenery we need for the stage.

We first performed the play eight years ago. At that time we used only mosquito nets for scenery. We hung a variety of nets upside down from the flies, pulling some of them at slanted angles. Depending on the lighting we employed, we could create complex and surprising effects, suggesting sometimes a forest, sometimes the bottom of the sea.

Eight years ago it was no particular trouble for us to assemble a sufficient number of nets. When we performed the play subsequently, we could supplement our original supply with nets obtained from friends and others close at hand. Now, however, we can't count on any household having even two or three of them. It seems that only older households still retain these nets. As time has gone on, it has become more and more difficult for us to find them.

The mosquito nets come in a variety of colors, but the most common ones are green with red edges, or variegated blue and white. For the purposes of the play, I liked the ones with the red borders, which somehow suggested something unlucky. Every time we hung these up, I began to wonder to myself why these nets were dyed green, and why they were always given red borders. How many homes in Japan, until lately, had been equipped with nets like these? I invariably posed these questions to myself, although no answers could be forthcoming. These will be the final performances of *The Trojan Women.* So I'll have to say goodbye as well to these two questions I've been living with for so long.

Betrayal

If I just sit on the stage day after day, I begin to feel unhealthy. So I've started to do my exercises along with the performers. Everyone joins in for an hour before rehearsal begins. The performers warm up their bodies in various ways, stamping their feet or going down on their knees, following along with the musical rhythm. They vocalize as well. Every day, with minor variations, they do a set of exercises that I have designed. I used to do all of this too, thinking that I might move myself around a bit and train my voice as well. Then I discovered something terrible. No matter how I worked my body, my voice always sounded awful. And if I didn't speak at all for a while, I could make no sound at all.

Ten years ago I had one turn at being an actor. We were invited to a theatre festival in France. In order to save on the transportation fees, I decided to play a role so as to reduce the number of people making the trip. During our three days of performances in Tokyo before our departure, a friend of mine repeated what one fan in the audience had said as he left the theatre: "That actor, whoever he is, has really undercut Suzuki's whole training method." That person evidently never suspected that it was me!

The creator of a method will, more than anyone else, undercut it in practice. But isn't that just what should happen with any set of theories about performance? I can preach my dreams precisely *because* I am incapable of carrying them out myself. I would be a rare performer indeed if I myself could bring my ideas to life. But still, I was glad that my own actors didn't say to me, "Why look, you don't seem to be able to keep good company with your dreams!"

Theatres Without Purpose

For the first time in quite a while, we're going out to perform in some of the smaller cities around the country. It is remarkable how the various prefectural halls and cultural centers resemble one another. All of them seem somehow not very well planned, and the actors find them unsuitable spaces in which to perform. I certainly can't complain about the fact that they are lavishly constructed and contain all the appropriate equipment. Yet the balance between such factors as the size of the theatre, the tones of its colors, or the relationship between the seats and the structure of the stage do not create a comfortable space for the body, a proper performing area. This kind of awkward space is probably only viable for making speeches with a microphone. It is not the kind of space in which an actor, using theatrical energies, can really create a sense of commonality with the audience.

Whatever is performed on this kind of stage thus becomes merely a spectacle. I worry over what the architects must have been thinking. If I asked one, he would doubtless reply that he designed a multi-purpose auditorium in accordance with the wishes of his patrons, and so it isn't any wonder that such a hall isn't really suitable for a live theatrical performance. A multi-purpose hall is really a hall with *no* purpose.

Japan has become an important economic power, and the cries of "Culture!" "Culture!" mount ever higher. This sentiment manifests itself these days in the desire to build big, pleasant, convenient halls. Since the time of the Greeks, however, whatever material progress has been made, the actor has continued to attract an audience on the basis of the force of his own physical energy. I can only hope that the search for convenience and pleasure that prompts the use of artificial energy will not kill that other form of energy, the one that only the body of the human actor can offer.

Actors and Those Big Radishes

These days we've gotten used to frogs and *daikon,* those long white Japanese radishes, in our own rehearsal hall. In fact, they play a crucial role on the very stage where I write and work.

The frogs don't actually appear on the stage; the actors seemingly become them. But the *daikon* appear in person. We eat them, quarrel with them, even kill characters with them. The big ones roll around on the stage, hang from the flies. At one point black ones seemed absolutely essential, so we began to paint the white radishes black, almost 200 of them. Well-shaped ones have something neat and pure about them; they reveal a sense of being that is somehow very touching. But when those pure and touching radishes are painted black, a terrible change comes over them. They appear then to be some kind of obscenity constructed from vinyl tubes. Hanging down from the rafters, tied with ropes near the base where the stems and leaves grow out from the root, there seems something weird and uncanny about them; they are almost like creatures from another planet.

I have never been particularly fond of eating cooked *daikon.* When they are boiled, they look somehow soiled and give the impression of being waterlogged. I prefer to eat them raw, cutting them into round slices with a knife and fork. They make a kind of crunching noise that I find quite endearing.

We have an expression in Japanese, something like "ham actor" in English: a clumsy actor is a "*daikon* actor." According to one theory, this expression comes from the fact that, no matter how you eat it, a *daikon* absolutely can't hurt you; in other words, they have no character, nothing to distinguish them. This explanation strikes me as strange. If these radishes show no special characteristics, they should be praised, not criticized. I'd like the term "radish actor" to become one of approbation. These days we have all too many actors who have so much personality they can make you very ill indeed.

Thinning Village

I met the mayor of Toga-mura, who has come up to Tokyo for a national conference of village mayors. I'm a citizen of his village, of course. He had a bit of spare time, so we had dinner together. The following day he planned to present a petition to the Ministry of Construction and then go back home, he said.

The various municipal authorities range from the governors of prefectures and mayors of cities down to the mayors of smaller towns and villages. The smaller the community, the worse its problems are. Of course, anyone who carries out the duties of a mayor, at any level, suffers hardships, whatever the particular circumstances. But the problems faced by the head of a village that is losing its population seem to call for new definitions altogether.

A mayor whose village is losing its population is faced with a desperate situation. He must try to improve the environment of his village as best he can, so that as few as possible of them will leave. All of village politics revolves around this one crucial factor. The mayor puts his efforts into redevelopment, encouraging local industry and the creation of a tourist trade. In one petition after another he seeks to ensure his sources of funds. Yet none of this can assure the success of his efforts to stop the exodus.

At the end of the war, Toga had a population of around 5,000. Now there are only about 1,200, and the outward flow has not stopped. As the number of inhabitants dwindles, the villagers begin to shake and tremble when even one more of them departs. Yet no matter how hard the mayor of such a town may work, there seems no way to stem the tide towards a city-centered society. Bringing a stop to such a trend would require an enormous change in the Japanese consciousness of how daily life should be lived.

Elsewhere I have explained the phrase, "to struggle on with the courage of the defeated." Here in this village, observing people for whom these words are literally true, I cannot help but be moved.

Place and Memory

It's been awhile, but I'm going to the theatre to see some performances by other troupes. When a play itself lacks interest, a forlorn atmosphere carries right on out into the audience. When I see a good production, however, I retain the memory ever afterwards of a warmth that seems to exude from the very ground on which the theatre is built. When I remember such an occasion, I think not only of the performance but of the street I took to get there, what and where I ate. Everything remains fresh and alive. Such experiences remind me of the way I felt about the theatre in the latter part of the 1960s, when the avant-garde performance groups began to emerge. I learned then that the work of a theatre troupe cannot be separated from the atmosphere of the place in which it performs.

As the media flourish in Japan, the theatrical world shows real vigor. When I first began working in the theatre, there was no information for the general run of spectators except what might appear in the newspapers. Little-known troupes only got mentioned if some friend of the group gave them a special write-up. Now there is radio, television, specialized magazines. When a particular production is even modestly accomplished, it gets royal treatment. Even if the big newspapers write nothing, the troupe won't suffer because of it.

The present boom in theatre construction is proof enough that this artform has earned its right to exist, at least as far as the younger generation is concerned. Yet because of the producer system, there seems little variety among the performances offered. No connections are established between theatre companies and the places where they perform. The accomplishment of an individual performer is something quite different from the force that a theatre group, a company, can exert. Thanks to the boom in building construction, the theatre seems at the point of dispersing the power of its greatest weapon, the concept of the theatre company itself.

Anticipating Next Year

It seems that early in January I'll be going to an international conference of theatre people in Calcutta. The special presentation that I'd planned for next year of *The Luncheon Party*—the new play I'm writing and directing—will have to be pushed up to the last days of this year, so the New Year's holidays will probably be frantic. Last year during that same period, I was in Togamura. But this time I won't be able to experience the tranquility of a whole day of watching the rabbits hop and skip over the snow.

My real hope is that I can find some remarkable performing spaces in India. When you meet theatre people, no matter how superb they are, all you can do is talk to them, which is not so interesting. But when a real theatre person comes in contact with some new stage or performing space, he doesn't have to *say* anything. A really fine stage will inspire in him a state of physical well-being. Will the coming year be a healthy one for me? India will decide.

K.N. Panikkar's group from Kerala, India will be coming to participate in our Toga Festival this summer. It is a small company which has been very encouraging to me. In their work they experiment with turning the physical sensations of traditional Indian theatre into a contemporary theatrical experience; in this respect, at least, their work resembles mine. They will present several of their works.

I have just begun to learn something about the state of the Indian theatre and there may well be some opportunity for our two companies to engage in some joint efforts. We greatly anticipate that occasion, and we'll welcome Mr. Pannikar at Togamura. Soon we'll be able to admire not only what the Americans are doing but what the Indians are doing as well.

7

A Play: Clytemnestra

I had thought for some time about trying to adapt the great Orestes legend from a contemporary point of view. The word "adaptation" may seem inaccurate—I have actually reconstructed the story, "requoted" it, as it were. Using the various Greek tragedies that involve the House of Atreus as my raw materials, I have attempted to put together a new story of Orestes that follows none of them exactly.

What I hope to portray in *Clytemnestra* is the age-old clash between the way in which people sustain the institution of marriage, and the real human relationships that develop within it. By examining closely the destruction of the family as a fundamental and basic unit, I hope to suggest something of the solitary state in which modern man now finds himself.

My fascination with the Orestes legend grew out of my interest in the issue of power, and how it shifted from women to men at the time when ancient Greek values were being rent asunder. But that was not the only thing that interested me in the legend. I had certain doubts concerning Orestes, who was driven to kill his mother; he seemed too abstract a human being to me, his attitudes merely emblematic, as though he were no more than a "sign" or fixed landscape. The legend of Orestes is based on incidents that actually did take place. Whatever the circumstances, however, when the story was codified in the playwright's words, turned into a drama which then became part of a larger cultural system, it no longer represented one individual human experience. Rather, it came to seem as if it had actually been constructed within the realm of general human ideas. I could not believe, for example, that a murderer, just after killing his mother, would say, "All of Greece will benefit from my act. Because I have done the deed and gotten rid of her, the unjust custom of wives killing their husbands will become obsolete." I do not mean that such a statement was a deliberate lie. But the cultural system that made such discourse possible quite surprised me. A similar inversion of logic can be noted in the argument of Apollo, who, in order to justify Orestes' murder of his mother, says, "The real mother is not necessarily the person who gives birth to the child. That woman only gives shelter to the unborn baby in her loins. It is the father who profits from the child. The mother merely brings up a child as a host would take good care of a guest." This sheer quibbling does acquire, however, a force of reality within the drama.

The fact that a man who has experienced such agonies can only take on the pallid existence of a figure in a landscape, and that a god who does not actually exist can spurt forth nonsense as a theatrical reality that pleases an audience, certainly suggests that, more than 2,000 years ago, Greek society had reached a level of ripeness rapidly approaching decadence. I believe that contemporary Japanese society strongly resembles that earlier situation. It was the significance of that resemblance that surprised me above all.

This *Clytemnestra* is the third Greek tragedy that I have adapted and produced. The first was *The Trojan Women,* which we initially presented at the Iwanami Hall in Tokyo, and the second was *The Bacchae,* which premiered at the Iwanami Hall and was then produced in America with a Japanese and English-speaking cast. *The Trojan Women* was written and conceived in a traditional style, while *The Bacchae* was developed in a Western style. This play, however, is my attempt—my idea is hard to express in words—to break through those other styles and create a play that shows the relationship between them. In comparison with the earlier plays, this one might thus be said to be conceived in a *contemporary* style. Characterizing the three plays in this fashion suggests, and rightly so, that I wish them to be performed in those three differing modes. I hope that together, the plays will suggest how that genre we refer to as the drama can intersect with contemporary society.

Bits of this play will seem quite familiar as you encounter them, but I have done my best to construct a play that, in its entirety, reveals a new dimension of reality.

Parts of my text come from the following six classic dramas: Aeschylus' *The Oresteian Trilogy;* Sophocles' *Electra;* and Euripides' *Electra* and *Orestes.*

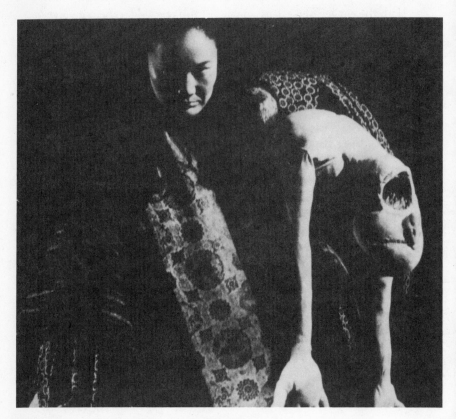

Clytemnestra, Scene Four

PROLOGUE

Before the King's palace. ELECTRA *in the center, surrounded by the*
     CITIZENS.
CITIZENS: In this world,
     You are not the only one
     Who has suffered, Electra.
     Your rage to suffer,
     Compared to what others have suffered
     Is too severe,
     Even compared to poor Orestes,
     Sent off in all his sadness
     To spend his youthful days
     Hiding from men's eyes.
     Yet Orestes, surely,
     By the guidance of great Zeus himself
     Has returned to our own country.
     He is heir to the throne,
     And we must greet him gratefully.
ELECTRA: I have waited forlornly,
     Unceasingly,
     For his return.
     I have not married, I have no child,
     I am as I always have been,
     Poor, pitiful Electra.

CITIZENS: Gather your strength, Electra.
    Zeus, in the heavens, powerful as ever,
    Discerns all that transpires
    In this world.
    Do not grieve too much.
    Time is the kindest of the Gods;
    As a keepsake of renowned
    Agamemnon,
    Orestes, from the beginning,
    Even at the holy river, known also to the Gods,
    Never forgot his enemy.
ELECTRA: Yet I see the months, the years
    Pass by empty, endlessly,
    Without hope.
    No strength remains to me.
    I have lost my parent
    And I am lost as well
    In thoughts of vanishing away;
    I have no husband to protect me
    With his shield,
    And, like some nameless, floating creature,
    I am treated as a servant in my father's own home,
    Wearing these miserable rags,
    Facing my meager table.
CITIZENS: That painful cry at the time of coming home,
    Both blades of the bronze battle axe
    Coming down on your dear father's forehead,
    That terrible cry as he struggled up from his banquet seat:
    It was Cunning that planned this,
    And the work of Unrighteous Love.
    It was the pair of them that gave birth
    To this bewitching shape,
    A god? A human being?
    The one who could perform
    Such a vile deed.

ELECTRA: That day,
    More than any other day,
    How hateful that day was to me.
    It revolts me
    Even to bring that evening
    To my lips:
    That fearful curse
    Rising up from the banquet seat,
    My father's ghastly end
    Brought about by the pair of them.
    Now those two pairs of hands as well
    Set to work against me,
    Now nothing can save me.
    O Zeus,
    May this pair
    Be made to suffer
    For the crimes they have committed,
    May as great a crime be done to them,
    Drunk on their pride and glory.
CITIZENS: Stay, go no further, Electra.
    True, for some reason or other
    You must meet with such misery;
    Yet your soul grows ever blacker,
    You go from one struggle to another,
    Bringing on yourself an ever worsening fate.
    You need not suffer.
    You should never have quarreled
    With those who hold power.
ELECTRA: There was nothing for me to do
    But meet with these horrors, these horrors.
    I know myself: I am stretched taut,
    Yet whatever misfortune I may meet,
    How can I cease my lamenting
    As long as I am alive?
    There seem to be none among you

Who understands my plight
And truly knows what to say to me.
I am grateful that you try to calm me,
Yet you will leave me as I am.
Nothing now can save me
From the abyss in which I find myself.
It is for this reason that I lament unceasingly;
There never will be a time when my sufferings will stop.

CITIZENS: You speak with the faithfulness
Of a mother thinking of her child;
Yet we beg you,
Do not pile one misfortune upon another.

ELECTRA: A simple misfortune is nothing
Compared to this.
What to do,
When a person turns away from the dead
As though he knew them not?
I do not think that such a person should be praised;
And should I happen to meet with some good fortune,
I could not, in the face of what has happened to my parent,
Meet with any happiness
Until there were no more cause for me
To continue my lamenting,
Crying out until my very voice itself
Seems wrung from me.
The one who kills another,
Even should he not receive
Just retribution for his crime,
Must still feel the shame of men,
Fear of the Gods,
And so he must disappear,
Vanish away.

QUEEN CLYTEMNESTRA *appears in the center door. She is
followed by serving maids who carry offerings.*

CLYTEMNESTRA: I see you are still prowling about out here, just as proud as ever. Aegisthus is away. Otherwise, you would never go around bringing shame on our House in this fashion. Now that he has departed, you seem to give no consideration at all to me. You often say that I am an impudent woman, and there are rumors spread abroad that you are badly treated. Yet I have absolutely no evil intentions in mind. I always hear from you what a monster I am, yet I say very little about you in return.

You seem to harp on nothing but the fact that I helped to kill your father. Well, I did kill him, and with my own hands. I do not resist your saying this. Nor was your father killed with my strength alone. The Gods of Righteousness performed the deed. They lent their hands because they became the allies of Justice. Your dead father, whom you have never stopped making such a fuss about, made a sacrifice to the Gods of your own sister, whose blood you share, as if it were nothing. When that child came into the world, he never had to suffer the pangs of birth the way I did. So tell me, please. For what reason did your father sacrifice your sister? Do you think it was for the sake of the Greeks? They would not have been capable of demanding such a sacrifice. Your father did this out of cruelty, saying it would help win in the battle against Troy. You may have some different idea, but this is what I believe. And if that dead child could speak herself, she'd say the same. So I am not ashamed one bit for what I did. If you think I am wrong, then think what you please. But look at the situation as it is before you go about blaming other people.

ELECTRA: But why, Mother, did you do such a thing, which even now brings shame down upon our House? Tell me, why? You slept with the man, the murderer with whom you joined forces to kill my father—you even had a child by him—then thrust your other children away from you and would not even take them in. When I see such conduct, why should I remain silent and say nothing? And do you say I pursue a path of revenge, one that was snatched away from my sister? If such is what you wish to spread abroad, Mother, then your words are shameless indeed. It is absurd for you to say that what you did was for your daughter, that your husband was your enemy, that what you did was a fine thing. You always complain loudly that I revile you, my living mother, yet how dare you reprove me? For I, who pass day after day in misery and am treated so cruelly by you and by your consort, think of you as my master, not my mother. And there is another, too, my poor brother Orestes, who barely managed to escape from you and who manages only to eke out some frugal existence in a distant land. You never cease to blame me for the fact that I brought him up wanting nothing but to seek vengeance for the death of his father. I want you to understand that, if I myself had the strength, that is just what I would wish for. Say to the world of me and my actions what you will—that I am an evil woman, that I shout abuses, that I know no shame. For if I were accomplished in all such things, then I could show myself not unworthy to be your daughter.

CLYTEMNESTRA: What a brazen girl you are. Whatever I am forced to say to you becomes *my* fault, all my fault, whatever I may do.

ELECTRA: It does you good to hear abusive language. For just now your luck seems good.

CLYTEMNESTRA: And neither you nor Orestes can stop it. *(She turns to her serving maids)* Now is the time to offer prayers to the Gods to rescue me from the fears that seize me. Hold high aloft and present the offerings of fruits and nuts that have been piled here.

Apollo, the God who protects us from ill-fortune, please listen to these words, confused and full of riddles as they are, which I offer up to you. All who are with me here are not my friends, my allies. This very daughter here beside me does not hesitate, clinging to her hatred, to spread vile rumors about me in every corner. So I may not speak completely freely to you. Listen to my words as they are, and try to understand.

I had a dream last night that might have two meanings. Apollo, if the dream was a good dream, let it come true. But if the dream was truly an evil one, may it devolve upon my enemies instead. And although there are those who would seek to rob me of my happy state in life, may you never allow it. Permit me to live on, quietly and peacefully as I do, protect the home and crown of the House of Atreus, and bring happiness to my consort, as well as to those of my children who do not detest or curse me. Apollo, please give me a sign that you have heard my prayers. Please grant for me, for all of us, the supplications I have made to you. And other things as well, which I have not spoken of: try to understand them in your sacred person. For you, a son of great Zeus himself, can forsee all.

ELECTRA (*Extending her right hand in a gesture of prayer*): To the Gods of this world and, above all, to the sacred messengers of the Gods from the other world who are among them, I have a request for Hermes, who resides in that universe below us. May the sacred spirits who live under the earth now hear my prayer. I call to the spirit of my departed father. Look on me and on my poor brother Orestes with pity. May we somehow or other become Masters of our House again. For our own mother has put Aegisthus in your place, the two of them having plotted to kill you as they did. They did the same to those who served you and, taking away his patrimony from poor Orestes, they chased him away to live in another land. They have performed every possible atrocity. All the riches that you gathered together so painstakingly, they have used as they liked for their own prosperity. May Orestes somehow find his way back to this land and, through some happy course of events, my dear Father, may my prayers be answered; may Orestes be the harbinger of our happiness in this life. May all this come about through the Gods in their strength, through the might of this great Earth itself, and by the victory that righteous judgment will bring.

SCENE ONE

A room in a temple. In the rear, statues of Apollo and Athena are symmetrically arranged. ORESTES *is sleeping before the statue of Apollo.* ELECTRA *gazes intently on him.* ORESTES *opens his eyes.*

ORESTES: I can sleep. You have calmed me, eased my cares. How grateful I am. When I needed you, you came to help. How kind you are. And you Goddesses, who helped me to forget my troubles, how wise you are, and how those unlucky ones like me wait anxiously for you. But how long have I been here? How did I come here? I cannot remember. I have forgotten altogether everything that has happened until now.

ELECTRA: My beloved brother. I am so grateful that you slept so soundly. So then, shall I help you to rise?

ORESTES: Yes, help me up. And wipe away all those excrescences that cling to my face.

ELECTRA: It is done.

ORESTES: Support my body; place me sitting up, straight. And push my matted hair away from my face. It bothers me, I cannot see.

ELECTRA: The hair on your head is very dirty too. No comb has touched it for such a long time.

ORESTES: Let me lie down now and rest again. Now that my confusion dies, my strength dies with it, and my body can no longer respond.

ELECTRA: There, that seems better. One who is sick should rest. A sick bed may displease you, but now you must lie quiet.

ORESTES: Please lift me up again, then face me another way. The body of a sick man cannot move just as it pleases. How terrible to have to carry out all that I ask, one thing after another.

ELECTRA: Don't you wish to put your feet on the ground and try to rise by yourself? It has been so long. Wouldn't you like to try to walk, just a little? If you try to change your spirits, you will feel the better for it.

ORESTES (*Rising and trying to walk*): Yes! Yes, you are right. As I try, I can somehow feel my strength returning. I know that I am not yet well, but this feeling, this feeling is superb.

ELECTRA: Now that the Furies have brought you back to reason, please listen to what I have to tell you.

ORESTES: Have you something to tell me now? If what you want to tell me is good, I will be happy. But if it is bad, I have already heard enough. And dear sister, you must not become wicked, like the others. You must become quite different from them. Please, I beg of you. I don't just say this as some kind of pretext. I speak from the bottom of my heart. I plead with you. I beg you. And for you, Mother, I have a demand as well. Do not incite those daughters of yours on me, snakes stained in blood. Ah, they come toward me! They spring on me! (ELECTRA *hugs the overwrought* ORESTES *and tries to put him back in bed*)

ELECTRA: Poor, poor Orestes. Try not to be afraid. Get into your bed. You say that you see clearly, but all this is in your imagination. There is nothing.

ORESTES: The Furies, their eyes are like those of gloomy dogs. They would kill me! The priests who guard the dead in the underworld would kill me. . . .

ORESTES *tries to shake free from her arms.*

ELECTRA: Please don't try to speak. I will not let you thrust yourself about, so full of anguish; I will hold you tight with these two arms.

ORESTES: Speak! You, you too are one of those Furies and would follow after me. (*He pushes her away*) Give me the horned bow, a gift from the great Apollo himself. He told me that when the Furies frighten me and twist my thoughts, I could chase them off with this bow. (*Taking it in his hand, he*

[133]

strikes a pose as though shooting) Ah, disappear! For if not, even a God can be shot by the hand of a man. Do you not listen to what I say? Why do you fumble and hesitate? Set wings aflutter, skim the great sky, and urge on the divine oracle of Apollo. *(Waking from his madness)* Sister. Why do you hide your face with your hands and weep? With my illness, I cause you pain and trouble. I dare not show myself to you, who must become companion to my suffering. Yet you must not weep at my misfortunes. You have been virtuous. It is I who killed our mother. And it is I who blame Apollo. For he tempted me, and led me to carry out such a disloyal act. Pretending to bring us joy, in reality he did nothing for us. If I could meet our father, and could ask him if I should have murdered my mother, he would surely reply, "She is the woman who gave birth to you. How can you pierce her throat with a sword?" Yet in truth, even though I have slaughtered my own mother, I have met with bitter days and am filled with remorse. But that is all over now. My father will never come back to life again. Ah, my poor, pitiful sister. Because of me you have not slept. Now close your eyes. Please eat, and bathe yourself. For it would be the worst thing of all if you should collapse or fall gravely ill yourself. As you know so well, everyone has abandoned me. You are the only one on whom I can depend.

ELECTRA: Do not fear. I will never abandon you. We shall live and die together. And if you should die, what, after all, would happen to me, a poor woman? I have no brothers, no father, no friends to whom to turn. If you think it good then, let us rest now. Yet as you lie down, do not be frightened should something try to drive you away. Rest, rest without stirring. A person who is well, if he thinks himself sick, will end in suffering.

ELECTRA *leaves.* ORESTES *stares vacantly in front of himself. Suddenly the* FURIES *appear, as if out of the heavens. They look down on* ORESTES. *As they do so, the statue of* APOLLO *at the rear brightens and begins to move.)*

SCENE TWO

The internal conflicts that ORESTES *feels now spin themselves out in a violent give-and-take between* APOLLO *and the* FURIES.

APOLLO: I certainly have never abandoned you. I have unceasingly remained at your side and bestowed my protection upon you. It was the same, even when we were far apart. There was certainly no great God who held any animosity toward you. And as for these revolting women, neither any God, nor any human being, nor even a beast has any contact with them. For the evil that they have brought forth, they will live in foul darkness, under the ground in the dankest hell, where they will earn the hatred of men and Gods alike. In any case, now is the time for you to flee. Do not falter in your resolve, for they will pursue you as far as they can. Across the wide land, in any country where you may wander, even across the seas, to far towns by the floating waves. Keep well this suffering in your heart, but do not be discouraged. *(He rises and faces the* FURIES, *who look down from the heavens)* Flee from here. I order you. Leave this spot at once. The place where you live is a land where executioners dwell, a spot where men's eyes are gouged out, their throats slit, where future generations are cut off, where children are violently abused, their hands and feet cut off, where victims are buried alive and run through with stakes while they scream themselves to death. Leave. Leave here at once. There is no shepherd to look after your roaming flock. There is not one God who would give service to such a body of beasts as you.

FURIES: Listen to what we have to tell you, for all of this is your responsibility. All of this happened because of *you*.

APOLLO: What do you mean? Tell me only the reason.

FURIES: You acted as the oracle who told him to kill his mother.

APOLLO: I only told him to strike his father's enemy. And what of that?

FURIES: And now it is you who agrees to condone the spilling of new blood.

APOLLO: And that is why I told you to flee this place.

FURIES: Now you tell us that you reproach us?

APOLLO: Because it is not becoming for you to appear here.

FURIES: Yes, to pursue is the duty we have been given.

APOLLO: Duty indeed. What do you mean by that? What an exalted assignment. How proud you must be of yourselves.

FURIES: We pursue from place to place one who has done harm to the mother who bore him.

APOLLO: But what of the wife who killed her husband?

FURIES: That offense is different from the harming of one's own flesh and blood.

APOLLO: Yet in marriage, of all ties, the husband and wife are bound together in an oath, so that their all-important fates are linked as one, defended by Right and Virtue. Yet, should the husband kill the wife, or the wife the husband, you would forgive the crime, quite overlook it, and not regard what you saw with angry eyes. If that is so, it can by no means be said that you are right to pursue Orestes to one land after another. On one hand you are intense, on the other, you seem slipshod. In any case, Athena will judge the merits of this case.

FURIES: Whatever you say, we will never give up this man.

APOLLO: So you will pursue him as you will. Why such a fruitless effort?

FURIES: Please do not hinder us in our duty.

APOLLO: Indeed, I would not dream of taking such a responsibility from you!

FURIES: In any case, it is by the power of Zeus, in all His majesty that, because a mother's blood was spilled, we, like hunters, pursue this man who deserves a righteous punishment. The blood of a mother, once spilled, cannot flow back into her body again. Water dashed on the ground is gone forever. We will drag you off, Orestes, to a dry and stony hell. Such will be your punishment for having killed your mother. *The* FURIES *vanish.* ORESTES *clutches himself in fright.*

SCENE THREE

ELECTRA *drags along the dead body of* AEGISTHUS *and throws it down in front of* ORESTES. *He is amazed.* ELECTRA *grips a pointed knife.*

ELECTRA: Ah, what a glorious victory. Orestes, you are indeed your father's son, our father who revealed his superb exploits in the battle for Troy. And this odious Aegisthus, who murdered our father, now he has been slain as well.

ORESTES: We must first look to the Gods. It is through the Gods above all that such good fortune has come to us. And next, perhaps it is I who should be praised. For I acted as the servant of fate, and of the Gods as well. I am the one who actually murdered Aegisthus. All of this is no longer idle talk. Use this carcass as you will. Give it to the wild beasts for food, or provide it as bait for the birds of the air. Let it bleach in the fields; pierce it with a stake to hold it fast. Whatever you like. This body is your slave. Before, it was your master.

ELECTRA: There is something that I must say to you, and yet . . . I hesitate.

ORESTES: Why do you hold back? Say what you will. Now there is no reason to fear.

ELECTRA: I find myself ashamed to speak of it before this corpse. For there surely will be those who will hate me.

ORESTES: There is no one at all who would speak badly of you.

ELECTRA: Yet in this city, there are many who are peevish and ready to speak ill.

ORESTES: Sister, if you have something to say, say it. In the hatred we felt together for this man, there is a terrible sadness we never planned for.

ELECTRA: Say nothing more. *(To the body)* It is you who have engineered my destruction. You have stolen away my beloved father. You have made orphans of my brother and myself. Yet we had done nothing to harm you. And you married our mother, in the most shameless fashion. The lord you murdered was the great general of all the armies of Greece. Yet you yourself never went to fight in that terrible battle for Troy. What a fool you were! You married my mother, soiled the bed that should have been my father's. You hoped that the wife you had waited for would always be true to you. You should have understood! *(She stabs the body with the knife she is holding)* Anyone should know how foolish it is to commit adultery with another man's wife and then be enticed into marrying her. Especially if he thinks that she will remain faithful to him. What a sad life you have had. You have suffered more agony than anyone. *(She begins to cut his penis with her sword)* You felt that your marriage was an immoral one, because you knew that when my mother took you as her husband, you had taken on a bad master. Everyone, all over Greece, said this of you. You are a man who is a woman, they said, yet the woman is never called a man. How unseemly all this is. The master of the house a woman, you not the real husband. The children were disgusted; here we were, born in this place, yet we could not be called by our father's proper name. To take your name from your mother. How disgusting. It must seem strange that I, an unmarried woman, speak of your dealings with women. But from whatever vantage point I speak, you understand all too well what I am saying. You did terrible things. You made use of the fact that you lived in the palace, and you took pride in your good looks. But I detest a man like you, who has a womanish face. A husband should be a manly person. When a child is born, he can show off his good looks when he weaves garlands of flowers for the dance. That is all. Well, you understand by now, I think. What of your crimes has been detected, and what punishment must you suffer? When a man carries out successfully the first step of any scheme, he must not think that he can then win out altogether over the justice of the Gods. For until the very end, until his life is over, he can never know for sure. (*She stabs the body again and again.* ORESTES *is terrified*)

ORESTES: Sister, stop this. You must stop.

ELECTRA: Ah! What do you see over there?

ORESTES: The mother who gave us birth.

ELECTRA: Exactly so. Somehow her chariot and her clothes seem to be glittering with light. She has brought her entourage along.

ELECTRA *and* ORESTES *drag the mutilated body out of sight.*

SCENE FOUR

To the sound of eerie music, the FURIES *and the* CITIZENS *appear, waiting for* CLYTEMNESTRA. *In a moment she comes in, dragging the bodies of the just-murdered* AGAMEMNON *and* CASSANDRA. *The scene is from the memories of* ORESTES *and* ELECTRA.

CLYTEMNESTRA: What was said to me there before, and what you may say against me now, bring no feelings of shame to me at all. When I devised my plan, facing enemies who pretended to be friends, I set up no ordinary trap: I wanted the enemy to be captured, allowing no escape. I decided on such a compact long ago, on the day when our quarrel first arose. For it is I, who could not forget that ancient argument, who have done this. This act has been a long time in coming. But as all of you can see, it is I who stand beside those I have struck down, and I have done as I planned. I have no intention of concealing anything. I threw a net over him like a fish; he could not flee, escape his fate, or slip away. I pulled him about madly, struck him twice so that he let out two screams, then slumped down. And there, where he fell, I struck him a third time. He fell over then, and took in his last breath. Blood spurted from the gashes in his mouth. Black blood splashed over my body. Yet I was as happy as if it had been a blessed rain falling from Heaven. So it is that I wish all of you assembled here to rejoice with me. For this is my moment of exaltation.

CITIZENS: We are shocked and surprised at these words you utter. How brazen you are. How boastful you sound, speaking thus of your lord and husband.

CLYTEMNESTRA: You all despise me as a woman who cannot tell right from wrong, and you would test me. Yet I am fearless, and I speak to those who would understand me. If you praise me or blame me, it is all the same. That is my husband, Lord Agamemnon, now a corpse, brought to a finish by the deed of my own right hand, in a skillful act of Righteousness. So be it.

CITIZENS: Woman, how could you have caused such violence that all here turn against you, the object of our cruel hatred? You must be banished from this place.

CLYTEMNESTRA: You want to drive me from the city? Yet before this, you did nothing against *him!* When he sacrificed his own daughter, the sweetest child born of my own flesh, made a sacrifice of her to pacify some Thracian wind. It was *he* whom you should have driven away, for the foul disservice he did toward the Gods. Yet you will judge my deeds. Let me tell you that I am prepared for any sort of threat. If I am driven from here, I will win the contest. Better to let me go free.

CITIZENS: You speak as though you have lost your reason. Your spirit is deranged because of your acts of murder; now, both your eyes seem smeared with blood. You must atone for what you have done.

CLYTEMNESTRA: Listen carefully to me. A man has fallen who has disgraced the woman he called his wife. He seduced many of the women he found at Troy. And that Cassandra, the captive he brought from there, who served as his nurse, who interpreted the oracles: she was the faithful guardian of his bedroom, she occupied a seat on his boat. The crimes of these two could not have gone unpunished. The man behaved as I have told you. And the woman, like a swan, sang a sad song that announced her death; now she sleeps beside him like a child. As for me, I brought her home from that lavish banquet like some special garnish.

CLYTEMNESTRA *stands astride the dead body. Her serving women appear. Pieces of naked flesh are piled on their trays. They present them to the* CITIZENS, *one by one. The* CITIZENS *are horrified.* ORESTES *and* ELECTRA *look on.*

SCENE FIVE

ORESTES: What should we do with our mother? Must we really kill her? Truly?

ELECTRA: You've really lost your nerve, haven't you? Just because you saw her?

ORESTES: She's despicable. But still, why do we have to kill her? However hideous a mother she may be, she bore me and brought me up.

ELECTRA: Just why do you think this woman did away with our own father?

ORESTES: Ah, Apollo! Why was your oracle so foolish?

ELECTRA: Yet if Apollo was mistaken, then who is wise?

ORESTES: Making a prophecy to kill your own mother! Whoever you think may have done it, that kind of deed cannot be permitted.

ELECTRA: But what can hinder you from attacking the enemies of your father? (*She passes her knife to him*)

ORESTES: From now on, we will be accused of the crime of killing our mother. Yet until this day, I have never committed any act that was unclean.

ELECTRA: But if you did not defend your father, you would go against the will of the Gods.

ORESTES: Yet to accomplish what I must, I must take on the crime of murdering my mother.

ELECTRA: Yet if you abandoned your revenge for the death of our father, then what crime would you commit, and against whom?

ORESTES: Perhaps the one who spoke through the oracle was a monster, an apparition disguised as a God.

ELECTRA: I don't believe that for an instant.

ORESTES: I cannot believe that the oracle was without fault.

ELECTRA: You're losing your nerve, your manhood. That cannot be permitted. (*She pushes on him the blood-smeared body of* AEGISTHUS)

ORESTES: I'll do it. But I am taking a terrible duty upon myself. And I shall perform a frightening deed. If such is truly the will of the Gods, then there is no help for it. What a bitter contest this will be. There is no virtue in it. (*He throws the body of* AEGISTHUS *close to the feet of his mother*)

ORESTES: Mother!

CLYTEMNESTRA: Oh! What should I do! And you are dead, my sweet Aegistheus. Ah!

ORESTES: So you loved that man, did you? Then I can put both of you in the same grave. Once you are dead, you can never be betrayed again.

CLYTEMNESTRA: Wait! Please wait! Orestes, be scrupulous, tremble at what you may do. Remember who I am. My own child! You, who clung to these breasts! You nibbled on them in your sleep as I held you, drinking your fill of my delicious milk!

ORESTES: I shall now take your life, as you stand beside that man. While he was alive, you said that he was a better man than our own father. That's what you thought. Once I've killed you, you can go right on sleeping with him. You are still wild about him, aren't you? So of course you have come to hate the one you are supposed to love.

CLYTEMNESTRA: I am the one who brought you up. I would like to grow old with you as well.

ORESTES: After killing my father, do you think that we could live together?

CLYTEMNESTRA: All those things are decreed by the Fates. You, my dear, merely help them out.

ORESTES: If that is so, then it is the same Fate that is helping with my final preparations.

CLYTEMNESTRA: So then, you don't even fear the curses of your own mother?

ORESTES: I think of how my own mother, unluckily, thrust me away.

CLYTEMNESTRA: It isn't a question of thrusting away. I sent you off to the house of an ancient relative.

ORESTES: Even with such a glorious father as I had, I was sold twice over.

CLYTEMNESTRA: If that is true, where is the money? And who received it?

ORESTES: How humiliating, that I must be so blunt to censure you in this way.

CLYTEMNESTRA: You need not feel so. But by the same token, you must recognize the errors your father has made as well.

ORESTES: How horrible to speak ill of one who struggled in the world, difficulties piling up on him, while you sat at your ease at home.

CLYTEMNESTRA: A woman suffers as well when she lives apart from her husband for so long.

ORESTES: Yet it is the man who, by making his way in the world, affords the woman her livelihood, even if she sits by the fire.

CLYTEMNESTRA: So whatever your own mother does, you're going to kill her.

ORESTES: Yes. You, as far as I am concerned, are really murdering yourself.

CLYTEMNESTRA: Take care. Beware that the curse of my hatred does not pursue you like some monster.

ORESTES: My father's curse, and that of the Furies—how could you be saved, even if you could stop them?

CLYTEMNESTRA: You blubber useless words.

ORESTES: The fate of our father has brought this death upon you.

CLYTEMNESTRA: What did I do to give birth to, to bring up, such a viper?

ORESTES: Your fright over a dream—your worries have turned out an accurate prediction. When a man is murdered who should not be, then a terrible punishment must likewise be exacted.

ORESTES *pursues* CLYTEMNESTRA, *stabs her, and kills her. The* CITIZENS *flee in a group. The* FURIES *laugh in exultation.* ORESTES *stands, staring vacantly into space.*

SCENE SIX

The Goddess ATHENA, *who has been sitting without moving, rises and comes forward. The scene shifts to a court of law. What follows is a projection of what passes through the consciousness of* ORESTES.

ATHENA: What goes on here? Who are you that seek me out, all together in this fashion? You who come from another land to kneel before my statue, you who do not seem to belong to any human race of men. There are no beings like you among the Gods, and you have shapes that cannot possibly be considered human. Still, I cannot simply lay the blame on you. There would be no logic to that, it would fly in the face of Righteousness.

FURIES: We will explain as briefly as we can. We are children of endless Night, and we are cursed by all the families on this Earth.

ATHENA: I know your lineage, and how you are called in this world.

FURIES: Very well. Then listen to the duties we perform.

ATHENA: Tell me. But be precise in what you say.

FURIES: We drive away from their homes all those who have committed murder.

ATHENA: Yet where can the flight of those who have murdered find an end?

FURIES: Only in a place where the word "joy" is not in use.

ATHENA: And is it for such reasons that you hunt and pursue this man?

FURIES: Yes, for he is the one who set out to murder his mother.

ATHENA: Could this have been avoided? Or was there someone whose anger he had cause to fear?

FURIES: Is there any inducement so strong that it could drive a man to kill his mother?

ATHENA: Yours is one side of the story. There must be another.

FURIES: This man will take no vow from others, nor will he pledge himself.

ATHENA: It seems you do not seek the real truth but would be satisfied with what is said of it.

FURIES: What is this? Please explain what you mean. You speak in a complex fashion.

ATHENA: On the basis of a vow, Injustice must not claim the victory.

FURIES: So then, scrutinize carefully and render a just verdict.

ATHENA: Do you tell me that I may settle the case on the basis of the questions that I ask?

FURIES: Of course. We respect the power that you hold.

ATHENA (*To* ORESTES): Well then, what would you like to say concerning this matter? You, who come from another land. State where you have been, your lineage, and who you are. Then explain the charge against you. You came here as a petitioner, crouching in supplication near my altar, entreating my statue. Now, placing your faith in justice, answer each question put to you, responding as clearly as you can.

ORESTES: I was born in Argos and my father was the great Agamemnon, well known to you; he was the leader of those warriors who took to ships and, under Your divine protection, brought the citadels of Troy to ruin. Tragically he returned to his home, where he met his untimely end. His black-hearted wife murdered him, wrapped him in a hunter's net with her own hand. She killed her lord in his bath. Until now, I have lived away from my country; I returned to revenge the enemy of my dearest father. I murdered my mother. All of this came about through Apollo's intervention, for his oracle told me that if I delayed even an instant in seeking revenge against those who plotted to kill my father, I would be pierced to my very soul as punishment. Was my action virtuous or evil? It is for you to decide. I will submit to your judgment, whatever it may be. AGAMEMNON *and* CLYTEMNESTRA *appear. The play slips back into memory again.*

SCENE SEVEN

AGAMEMNON: My first duty is to pay homage at the shrine of the Gods, to thank them for our safe return and for the just revenge that we have wrought upon Troy. For those Gods lent us Their strength. The Gods have heard all: pleadings for justice that could know no dissent, revenge for warriors fallen in death, even the destruction of great Troy herself. Even now, that beleaguered, conquered city can be found by the smoke that rises from her. The winds of misfortune still blow. And with the dying ashes rise the last perfumes of bounteous luxury. So, let our profound thanks to the Gods stand as a sign of the enormous gratitude engraved forever upon our hearts. Our retaliation was carried out for an unseemly abduction; for the sake of one woman, Helen, a whole country was cast into ruin. And the famous colt whose emblem decorated the shields of our warriors sprang out from the depths of night, when even the stars had set. Leaping over the very walls of the forts like a lion eating at raw flesh, it licked the blood of Troy to its heart's content. Now let me proceed to the innermost recesses of my own palace, there first to pay homage to the Gods, those Gods who deigned to send us forth, then to bring us home. Victory has been with us until now. May there never be any change in this!

CLYTEMNESTRA: To all you citizens, to all you elders here assembled, let me tell you of those thoughts I have concerning my husband, for I have no hesitation to speak of them. As time passes, one's sense of reticence fades and disappears. I wish to speak of what I have learned from my own sad time of waiting, not what might have been gleaned from others' gossip. I will tell all that I have learned during that time my husband was in Troy. To be a woman and alone, waiting in a forlorn house, what a cruel and wicked thing that is. And more disturbing still to hear so many uneasy rumors. Messengers would come, one after another, to bear word of terrible hardship. If my Lord who now stands beside me had received as many wounds as those rumors had assigned him, he would have been more filled with holes than any net. The springs of tears that welled up in my eyes have run themselves dry; not even one drop remains. And these same eyes, sleepless from my helpless weeping late into the night, have remained red and swollen. When I could dream, even the tiny sound of some buzzing fly would be enough to wake me. And in those dreams, I saw you, Agamemnon, meeting with many more hardships than could transpire during the time in which I slept. Until this moment I have endured all; now, my heart, which had been lost to grief, can greet my Lord who stands before me. Like land appearing to sailors after a storm, this is a day of rejoicing for all the world. Is it not like a spring bursting forth, from which travelers may relieve their parched throats? How wonderful, that all this suffering can be set aside. I want to express in words all the joy I feel in my heart. And there must be no jealousy; we have suffered long enough. So then, my dear and longed-for Lord, come here to my side. Yet do not set your feet upon the ground, you who have defeated Troy herself. You maids who serve me, why do you delay? Do as I have told you and spread carpets on the ground where he will walk. Adorn his way with spreading purple. Let us greet our Lord properly. All other things, never lost in sleep, shall be managed with proper prudence.

AGAMEMNON: You have greeted me well and at great length after my long absence, you, the guardian of our House. Now it is just that others should speak words of praise. And do not heap luxury on me in your womanish fashion, nor prostrate yourself on the ground, nor call out to me open-mouthed, in a loud voice. And do not summon the envy of the Gods by spreading those robes upon the ground. For it is the Gods who should be praised for Their high glories. For me to walk upon this finery, a mortal man, makes me a bit fearful. I would be venerated as a husband, not a God. Even without these carpets to step upon, all of this beautiful embroidery, the world can praise me as fully as it will. The greatest gifts the Gods can give are just these scruples that keep us free from evil. A contented man is one who ends by meeting with the happiness he sought in this world.

CLYTEMNESTRA: I have yet one more thing to ask. Something truly from the heart.

AGAMEMNON: Ask, and I will not dissemble in my answer.

CLYTEMNESTRA: What if the king of Troy had performed your heroic deeds? What would he have done?

AGAMEMNON: He would surely have walked on beautiful brocades.

CLYTEMNESTRA: If that is so, why show any diffidence, why fear the criticism of others?

AGAMEMNON: The voices of dissent that rise from among the people can have a great force.

CLYTEMNESTRA: Yet one who earns no envy from others has nothing to be envied.

AGAMEMNON: To entreat a conflict does not become a woman or a child.

CLYTEMNESTRA: Yet radiant good fortune may sometimes give way.

AGAMEMNON: So then, in this dispute, you yourself seem quite resolved to gain the victory.

CLYTEMNESTRA: Grant this! For to yield gracefully is to win indeed.

AGAMEMNON: Well then, if you would really have me do so, let me walk upon this purple as far as the palace. Now, aside from this, I have brought with me this girl from Troy whose name is Cassandra. Take her to the palace and treat her properly. She was chosen as the brightest flower of Troy's vast treasures and so given to me by all the armies, as a gift. So then, let us go. *(He exits)*

CLYTEMNESTRA: There is the sea—and who can make the sea shrink up? In its depths are purple shells as valuable as any gold. And red juices throbbing forth. Such are the colors that dye these robes. My Lord, in our House, thanks to the Gods, there are many such things: we are not poor, we have only riches about us. As many robes could be put down as you might ever want. May the great God Zeus Himself deign to grant my wishes, and let all be decided in accord with Your Divine Will.

SCENE EIGHT

The scene reverts to the courtroom.

ORESTES *(Resuming his speech, exactly as before)*: I was born in Argos, and my father was the great Agamemnon, well-known to you, leader of those warriors who took to ships and, under Your divine protection, brought the citadels of Troy to ruin. Tragically he returned to his home, where he met his untimely end. For his black-hearted wife murdered him, wrapped in a hunter's net by her own hand. She killed her lord in his bath. Until now, I have lived away from my own country; I returned to bring revenge on the enemy of my dearest father, and I murdered my mother. All of this came about through Apollo's participation, for his oracle told me if I dallied even an instant in seeking revenge against those who had plotted to kill my father, I would be pierced to my very soul as punishment. Was my action virtuous or not? It is for you to decide. I will submit to your judgment, whatever it may be.

ATHENA: In such an affair as this, a judgment is too difficult for any man to make. Nor would I commonly pass sentence concerning a murder in which so much hate and rancor are involved. As the situation has come to this, however, I will select those who can judge these crimes, make them swear an oath for all eternity, and so establish a court of justice. Therefore, gather your proofs, and the words of your witnesses, each of whom can help respond to any objections. We will press for the truth in this case and make a decision. Remember your oaths, and let no one testify from any twisted motives. The trial now begins. (*To the* FURIES) Let all of you speak first, for the accuser must commence. The charges must be fully stated.

FURIES: There are many of us, but a few words will serve to explicate our case quite quickly. (*To* ORESTES) We wish you to answer our questions, one by one. First of all, did you murder your mother?

ORESTES: Of course I killed her. There's no denying it.

FURIES: And how did you kill her?

ORESTES: With sword in hand, I cut the nape of her neck.

FURIES: Who seduced you into doing this? Who contrived it?

ORESTES (*Indicating* APOLLO): It was at His urging.

FURIES: The oracle said that you should kill your mother?

ORESTES: Yes, and since then, I have never come to regret His help.

FURIES: When the sentence is handed down, you may feel differently.

ORESTES: I believe Him. And help, too, will come from beyond the grave. My father will send it.

FURIES: Believing in the dead comes from having killed your mother.

ORESTES: My mother was polluted with her crimes twice over.

FURIES: What do you suggest by this? Explain exactly what you mean.

ORESTES: On top of murdering her husband, she killed my father.

FURIES: Yet you still live. She can no longer be blamed for that murder.

ORESTES: Yet while she lived, why did you not pursue her?

FURIES: Because the man she killed was not related to her by blood.

ORESTES: Then it is I who am of her blood?

FURIES: You shameless murderer! She was your very own mother, who clasped you to her breast, gave you milk, and brought you up. You do not recognize the blood of your own mother?

ORESTES: So then, Apollo, bear witness Yourself and make the situation clear. It is true that I killed two persons. That cannot be denied. But make clear if what I accomplished in the light of Your wisdom was right or not.

APOLLO: In any case, the deed has been accomplished. No prophecy I have ever made could be deemed a lie; anything foretold from my holy seat, be it concerning man, woman, or a nation itself, derives from the will of Zeus Himself, the King of the Gods.

FURIES: So you are saying that it was Zeus who ordered this? That in order to avenge the murder of his father, Orestes need not have treated his mother with respect?

APOLLO: Certainly Agamemnon, this great warrior of high lineage, took from Zeus the scepter that gave him rule. The fact that his ever-glorious life was ended by the hand of a woman does not necessarily mean what it may seem. He could have died honorably, struck by an arrow when fighting the Amazons. That would have been a different case altogether. Athena, from what you have heard, you and your jury should listen to the circumstances and pass judgment on this case. For when Agamemnon finally came happily home from the wars, Clytemnestra welcomed him lightheartedly, invited him to the ritual bath; then, when the lustrations were about to be finished, she threw a robe around him, crowded in upon him, and struck her husband. Now you have heard how this great and awesome general, whose honor surpassed that of a myriad of others, ended his life.

FURIES: According to what you say, Zeus should have taken the best care of his own father, Cronos. Yet did he shelter and protect Him? You call forth a subterfuge. Remember, the one who poured blood on the ground spilled that very blood he shares—his mother's. And will he not go on living in his father's House? On what altar can he make sacrifice?

APOLLO: I will explain this now as well. And you yourselves will understand the truth of what I say. In reality, a mother is not, in fact, the real parent to the child. She is only the womb in which the seed is planted, which she helps to grow. It is truly the father who has the child; the mother merely tends to it as it develops, as she would a guest who stops at her inn.

FURIES: How the old laws are being rent apart! These slights will call forth our revenge! On this ground, mark you, poisons will spew out. Mothers shall be made barren. Leaves and branches alike shall wither. The citizens will suffer bitter thoughts as their offspring wilt and die. Be one with us,

Mother of the Night, protect our ancient glories!
ORESTES *hears this furious exchange between the Gods.*
Suddenly, from the rear comes the father of CLYTEMNESTRA,
TYNDAREOS. *He carries a parasol. The scene returns to reality,*
as in Scenes One and Three.

SCENE NINE

TYNDAREOS: Orestes. You have shown no solicitude for justice,
nor did you appeal to any human law. My daughter struck
your father a blow and he lost his life. No act more dreadful
can be imagined, and I have no intention of praising her for
it. Yet you should have called on our sacred laws, charged
her with murder, and driven her from this House. In that
way you would protect both yourself and the law, so
respecting piety, gaining fame, without bringing misfortune
on yourself. But because you yourself have killed your
mother, you have become worse than she was herself. There
is something I must inquire of you. Take the case of a wife
who shares her bed with her husband, then kills him. The
children of the murdered man then kill their mother. Next,
the child of those who committed the murder attacks the
murderers themselves. How far will such miseries extend?
Our ancestors found a way to deal with this. One who committed the crime of murder was forbidden to speak to anyone. His crime could incur only banishment; there was to
be no revenge by killing. Otherwise such murders would
continue on forever. Of course I detest shameless women,
and first among them my own daughter, who murdered her
own husband. I will continue to use every strength at my
command to force a stop to such murderers who, with their
bestial ways, destroy our city and our country. Orestes, you
evil knave! (*Hitting* ORESTES *with his umbrella*) When your
own mother bared her breasts to you and begged you to

[153]

help her, what did you feel then? I did not see the pitiful sight with my own eyes, but when I think of the terrible crime that you committed, these same eyes fill with tears at the ghastly sadness of it all. It is clear that you are hated by the Gods. You are wild with fear and loathing, all as a punishment for what you have done to your mother. This stands as proof enough. I have seen you with my own eyes. There is no need for me to seek other witnesses. True, my daughter should have been put to death. But you were not the one to kill her. I have been a happy man, except for my daughter. In that respect, I have been unlucky.

ORESTES: Honored one. As you have said, I am the man guilty of the crime of murdering my mother. This I know. Yet since I struck down the enemy of my own father, I do believe that I have committed no crime. There was nothing else that I could have done. To your charges, there are two rebuttals. First of all, my father planted the seed, and your daughter, receiving it, served as the field in which that seed was planted. She brought me up. Without a father, no child could be born. She took me, and grew me in her womb. Thus it was my father, more than my mother, who was the first cause of my life, it is he who put me into this world. Then, your daughter—I am ashamed to call her my mother—did make another pledge and took another man into her bed. When I say that she was wicked, I expose my own shame as well, yet this must be. Aegisthus, hidden in the palace, served as her paramour. For this reason I killed him, and sacrificed her as well. I know full well that I performed an immoral act, but it was carried out to avenge my father. For those two deeds, for those two deeds I have committed, you would have me hanged. But I would answer thus in response to your attempt to intimidate me. First of all, you must realize how much I have helped all of Greece by these acts I have committed. If women audaciously kill their husbands, then flee to their children and expose their breasts in order to seek sympathy from them, husbands will be attacked on any pretext. You proclaim loudly against me, but at least the terrible act I have committed will, as I said, make the repetition of such crimes impossible. I killed my mother because I hated her, and those feelings were justified. My mother betrayed her husband, who had gone to defend the nation, leaving her to guard the palace. She brought dishonor to the whole land. And, while knowing she had committed a crime herself, she, rather than accepting her punishment, thrust that punishment upon her husband, attacking my father and killing him. I know it is not auspicious to call upon the Gods when I myself have murdered. Yet as far as those very Gods are concerned, if I had acknowledged my mother's crime by silence, what would my dead father have done to me? You, Tyndareos, you of all people, who gave life to this loathsome creature, it is you who have ruined me. Because this audacious act of my mother made me lose my father, then turned me into a murderer! And look at the case of Apollo. Occupying a seat at the very center of the Earth, He dispenses to mankind the highest and brightest of all the oracles. And we humans, at the words of the God, must follow His directions. Thus I obeyed His commands and killed my own mother. If a mistake was made then it was made by the God, not by me. You must see *Him* as the immoral one, and you must hang Him. For there was nothing I could do. And if I must put the responsibility for this crime back on Him, has He no strength by which He can absolve Himself? If a God commanded my action, yet cannot rescue me from death, how can any man be saved?

What I did cannot be called unjust, yet you can say that it was unlucky for me that I did it. It is so that those among men who live in marital happiness can pass their lives in felicity; but when the life of a couple goes awry, they find themselves in an unlucky world, even within their hearth and home.

TYNDAREOS: You speak out boldly and with no circumspection, and your answers seem calculated to wound me. You make me want all the more to see you hanged. I came here to put flowers on my daughter's grave. And if you can be condemned at the same time, the occasion would be a fitting one indeed. I go now to the city assembly, where I will incite them all to decide to hang both you and that sister of yours. It would have been best to have hanged *her* long ago, in fact. She announced what Agamemnon told her in her dreams, how the Gods below the earth and everyone on the earth as well hated Clytemnestra; she told everyone of my daughter's misconduct with Aegisthus, repeating to you one thing after another, urging on your anger against your own mother until the whole palace was filled with the flames of cruel revenge. *(He strikes* ELECTRA*)* You are human trash. There is not one citizen who would take you as wife. It is exactly as you would expect. Who would marry a poor-looking woman, twisted and treacherous? For no one would want their children to be born as serpents! *(He faces the seated* APOLLO *and the statue of* ATHENA *at the rear. Then, as to the jury)* Do you listen? You would call yourselves new Gods, listen to what I advise, and carry out what I say. Do not suggest that death might be unfit for these two. Have the citizens put them to death by hanging. For if you do not do so, even if you name yourselves as Gods, you had best not set foot on the soil of this land again. *(He spreads his parasol and leaves)*

SCENE TEN

ELECTRA *weeps profusely. She looks intently into the distance while* ORESTES *stands, enduring all. The popular song "River of Fate" can be heard.*

Looking for a place / to get away tomorrow
I can't see with my eyes / River of Fate
Just as your love / flows right along
On that night of my consent / the rains came down

The love of us two / how hateful,
Those rumors turning bitter / River of Fate
From our old home town / on our trip, escaping
Is that a mountain? / the ocean?

Everything flows away / in the water
I don't want to live now / River of Fate
Your love: / even to the next life,
I want to follow you / I do.

ORESTES: Stop all that womanish crying, and try to bear the sentence as best you can. What a wretched business all this is. But we must somehow bear our fate. Don't go so far that you will kill me too. Monster that I am, I will be killed by my own countrymen, and that will be quite good enough. Don't give in to these disasters, please. Do not make me feel the coward, don't make me think on our own destruction and weep as well. This is the day on which we must face our deaths. The day when we must hang ourselves with a rope or sharpen our sword.

ELECTRA *takes a sword to cut her own throat.* ORESTES *stops her.*

It was enough that I killed my mother. I will not kill you. Kill yourself, by any means you choose. (ELECTRA *hugs* ORESTES) An embrace when you are facing death brings little joy, but do so if you find pleasure in it. You are the one who will put me at peace. And now it is I who wish to embrace you. Wretch that I am, I have nothing more to hide. Ah, my sister! Your breasts, I hug them tightly. You are my all. This embrace can take the place of marriage, of children. The two of us, lost in sadness, can at best call out to each other.

Electra. My sister. My sister. *(Clasped together, they fall to the ground in fierce pleasure)* I killed my own mother.

ELECTRA: I drew the sword.

ORESTES: To protect you, dear father.

ELECTRA: Nor did I ever betray you.

ORESTES: I beg you with tears in my eyes,

ELECTRA: And I, with lamentation,

ORESTES: Oh, Great Earth! And You, Zeus, who witnesses all things of men. Look on the end of these two abhorred murderers. By my own hand there will be two bodies lying layered on the ground. Such will be the compensation for my hardships. So then, Apollo, even if your self-proclaiming justice is only the most ordinary, the fulfillment of all this suffering will here and now be all too clear. Now those who murder will, by your strength, be banished from their good lives, chased from Greece. Yet it should not matter to what country I may go. Will any of the devout and pious of other lands look me, a murderer, in the face? You have seen for yourself. You have seen, in that grief before death, what a breast was like, naked, with the robes stripped away.

ELECTRA: And a voice that shrieks, ah! And a voice that asks, have patience.

ORESTES: This cannot be endured. For I took the hair of her head . . . grasped the robes above me, took my sword, and made her the object of my sacrifice. I thrust my sword deep into her throat.

The ghost of CLYTEMNESTRA *appears and slashes at the two with her knife as they embrace.*

ORESTES *(Gazing intently into the distance)*: Mother!

The dead bodies of ELECTRA *and* ORESTES *now lie stretched out in a corner of the temple. The lurking ghost of* CLYTEMNESTRA, *with the bloodstained knife in her hand, stares vacantly into the distance.*

CURTAIN